Neo-Race Realities in the Obama Era

Neo-Race Realities in the Obama Era

Edited by
Heather E. Harris

Published by State University of New York Press, Albany

© 2019 State University of New York

All rights reserved

No part of this book may be used or reproduced in any manner whatsoever without written permission. No part of this book may be stored in a retrieval system or transmitted in any form or by any means including electronic, electrostatic, magnetic tape, mechanical, photocopying, recording, or otherwise without the prior permission in writing of the publisher.

For information, contact State University of New York Press, Albany, NY
www.sunypress.edu

Library of Congress Cataloging-in-Publication Data

Names: Harris, Heather E., editor.
Title: Neo-race realities in the Obama era / edited by Heather E. Harris.
Description: Albany : State University of New York, [2019] | Includes bibliographical references and index.
Identifiers: LCCN 2018027994 | ISBN 9781438474151 (hardcover : alk. paper) | ISBN 9781438474144 (pbk. : alk. paper) | ISBN 9781438474168 (ebook)
Subjects: LCSH: United States—Race relations—21st century. | Racism—United States. | Post-racialism—United States. | Obama, Barack—Influence.
Classification: LCC E184.A1 N368 2019 | DDC 305.800973/0905—dc23
LC record available at https://lccn.loc.gov/2018027994

10 9 8 7 6 5 4 3 2 1

Contents

List of Illustrations — vii

Foreword — ix
    Amardo Rodríguez

Acknowledgments — xi

Introduction — xiii
    Heather E. Harris

Part I

1 Obama's Transformation of American Myths — 3
    Zoë Hess Carney

2 Transformational Masculinity and Fathering in the Age of Obama: *"Roses and Thorns"* — 23
    Shanette M. Harris

3 How Obama's Hybridity Stifled Black Nationalist Rhetorical Identity: An Ideological Analysis on His Two-Term Third-Space Leadership — 53
    Omowale T. Elson

Part II

4 "Who Gets to Say Hussein? The Impact of Anti-Muslim Sentiment during the Obama Era" — 75
    Nura A. Sediqe

5 The End of AIDS? A Critical Analysis of the National
   HIV/AIDS Strategy   93
   *Andrew R. Spieldenner, Tomeka M. Robinson, and
   Anjuliet G. Woodruffe*

6 The President Was Black, Y'all: Presidential Humor,
   Neo-Racism, and the Social Construction of Blackness and
   Whiteness   109
   Jenny Ungbha Korn

7 L'homme de la créolisation: Obama, Neo-Racism, and
   Cultural and Territorial Creolization   131
   Douglas-Wade Brunton

Notes   145

List of Contributors   147

Index   151

Illustrations

Figure 3.1	Convergence Spiral of Identity Complex for Black Nationalism.	64
Figure 3.2	Media-Generated Perceptions of Obama.	67
Figure 4.1	"Do You Believe President Obama Is a Muslim?"	77
Figure 4.2	Public Perceptions toward Religious Groups.	79
Figure 4.3	Countries of Origin.	83
Figure 4.4	Discrimination and Identity.	86

Foreword

Amardo Rodríguez

Our actions and decisions always have consequences and implications. This is why our actions and decisions matter. So when the United States finally elected and reelected a Black man to be President, this had many important consequences and implications. Heather Harris has put together an impressive set of essays that looks at some of these consequences and implications. The essays are organized around the notion of identity, specifically how identity is being negotiated and contested after the election and reelection of the first Black President of the United States. This volume promises to make an important contribution to various discourses about identity, which emerged after the election and reelection of Barack Obama.

Indeed, many contend that our first Black President was in no way our first Black President. He was supposedly our first biracial President. His father was just as Black as his mother was White. Compounding this identity controversy is the fact that our first Black President values convergence rather than divergence. He came to prominence claiming that, "There is not a liberal America and a conservative America. There is the United States of America. There is not a Black America, a White America, a Latino America, an Asian America. There is the United States of America." This convergence trope pervades his most popular speeches. However, to claim that there is no Black America or White America is to make believe that the people who constitute these two groups have the same history and deal with the same challenges and circumstances. This is false by any measure of comparison. Case in point, after full terms, the facts reveal that Black folks economically regressed across the board under the first Black President and the number of people in poverty exploded. Only the rich got richer. In fact, never before had so few become so rich.

So yes, identity matters because our actions and decisions have consequences and implications. How we choose to perceive, experience, and narrate ourselves, and how others choose to perceive, experience, and narrate us, matters. It especially matters in a society that is eager to be post-race, that wants to be convinced that after the election of the first Black President, race is now behind us. Post-race means valuing commonality ("There is only the United States of America) rather than diversity ("There is not a Black America, a White America"). We achieve this kind of commonality by masking and downplaying the diversity within groups, such as masking and downplaying the diversity in any Muslim community. We reveal this kind of commonality when we say that certain things are offensive to persons of a certain group, when in fact no group is ever of one rationality, one sensibility, one modality, one history.

Post-race also means privileging economics over politics, such as Jason Riley, author of *False Black Power*, calling for Black folks to focus on fiscal capital rather than political capital. Most of all, post-race means the end of history, as in the end of Black folks claiming that the legacy of over 400 years of slavery, Black codes, and Jim Crow still impacts the present. Simply put, post-race means emphasizing opportunity rather than history. If a Black man can now become President, then race—or any other kind of difference that was historically marginalized in the U.S.—supposedly no longer has any purchase, and thereby should no longer figure prominently in anything, including identity. From a post-race perspective, our focus should now be on taking advantage of the opportunities that are supposedly there for the taking, regardless of our race, religion, ethnicity, disability, sexuality, or nationality.

Identity must supposedly have nothing to do with history. However, when history is erased, difference is erased, merely another face in a Benetton poster. It means nothing. Challenges nothing. Threatens nothing. Opposes nothing. Stands for nothing. As such, in order for identity to matter, history must remain prominent, which means Black folks reminding this society that choosing to enslave and brutalize a group of people for over 400 years has consequences and implications, and these consequences and implications still linger. Collectively, the essays in this volume do an impressive job of revealing and documenting this important fact.

Acknowledgments

I am grateful to the Divine who inspires me and to my late mother, Mrs. Euralene Greaves Harris, whose spiritual presence, 40 years later, still comforts and supports me in good and challenging times. Always remembered. Always felt. Always loved.

A hearty and loving thank you to my family and friends, in Canada, the United States, and Barbados, including but never limited to my father, Mr. Ralph Harris; my brothers, Mr. Wayne Harris, and Mr. David Harris; Mr. Graham Prescod; my aunt, Mrs. Eugene Harper; my late Uncle Mr. Selbourne (Uncle Sonny) Greaves, and my late aunt Mrs. Wilma Braithwaite; my cousins, Ms. Lorna Ajala, Ms. Brenda King, Mr. Marcus Francis, Ms. Angela Harris, and my late cousin Mr. Michael Philip (Mr. Miguel); and my tribe of nieces, nephews, and godchildren; and Mr. Victor Ajala.

To my friends and support team, I express gratitude to Dr. Roy Reese, Dr. Robin Means-Coleman, Dr. Amardo Rodriguez, Dr. Carolyn Stroman, Dr. Mutsumi Takahashi, Mr. Reudon Eversley, Ms. Sandy Daniels, Ms. Deborah Medford, Mrs. Balencia Owens, Ms. Karen Carter, Dr. Deric Greene, and Ms. Lori Rubeling; my Howard University Professors, especially Dr. Melbourne Cummings and the late Dr. Lyndrey Niles who made my Howard journey possible; Sista Docs, Dr. Clover Baker Brown, Dr. Cherylann Charles Williamson, Dr. Laura Dorsey Elson, Dr. Diane Forbes Berthoud, Dr. Sharnine Herbert, and Dr. Kimberly Moffitt; and the late Mrs. Marlene Corley and Mrs. Rena Simms.

Thank you to my contributors for your unending commitment to, and enthusiasm for, this project.

To the State University of New York (SUNY) Press team, and especially to Senior Acquisitions Editor, Dr. Michael Rinella, and Senior Production Editor, Ms. Eileen Nizer, thank you for your guidance and encouragement during the publishing process.

To the reviewers, I am grateful for your thorough feedback. Thank you!

Thank you also to my students, friends, and colleagues at Stevenson University for your support.

Peace, love, and laughter.

Introduction

HEATHER E. HARRIS

We recognize that the excluded are never simply excluded and that their marginalization reflects and determines the shape, texture, and boundaries of the dominant order and its associated privileged communities. The identities of the latter are inevitably defined in opposition to, and as a negation of, the representations of the marginalized, and in certain respects, the outside is always inside . . . (Iton, 2008, pp. 3–4).

The interconnectedness of the marginalized and the dominant was portrayed in sharp focus during the two terms of Barack Obama's presidency. Although he self-identified as African American—accepting the Blackness of his Kenyan father as well as his experiences as a Black person born in the United States, he also embraced his biracial status as shown by his reverence of his White American mother and grandparents from Kansas. According to Harris (2010), ". . . he was deliberate in presenting himself and his presence as "normal," and multiculturalism as a practice as opposed to an ideal" (p. 73). Nevertheless, he understood that his body, his presence, and his primary identity would be read as Black in order to fit the country's historical grand narrative and place him in an inferior space. A space that included marginalized others even though Obama occupied what many perceive as the most powerful position in the world—President of the United States of America.

His novel presence in the highest office in the land impacted not only the representation and negotiation of his intersecting identities but also the representation and negotiation of the intersecting identities of the citizens and residents of the United States. As a nation, we grappled with the dissonance created by having as our president a member of one of the most historically disdained and disenfranchised groups in the country, while simultaneously hoping that his tenure would serve as a positive turning point in race and identity relations. Although there were some changes as a result of Obama's policies, such as the Lilly Ledbetter Fair Pay Act, the Affordable Health Care Act, and the President's support of same-sex marriage, one change that never manifested was the post-race moment. Squires (2014) pointedly states: "That some were surprised at the post-election expressions of White racism and xenophobic nationalism is indicative of the failure of our society to further interrogate the collective memory of racial subjugation and to take accountability for the lasting effects of racial apartheid . . ." (pp. 194–195). The post-race aspiration had no foundation to build upon in an America that refuses to examine why it exists in its current form. Hence, when Obama's tenure began, rather than being perceived as a healing balm for the nation, his presence in the White House served to peel the bandage off of the country's infected and festering racial wound. It became clear that the deep cleaning required to facilitate our healing would not be forthcoming in the eight years or afterwards. In fact, I would add that in order to heal, we would have to be aware of what I propose as the Whiteness Conundrum—namely the intertwining of White supremacy, White privilege, and White indifference that often results in discriminatory policies and practices being applied in a nonchalant fashion. This conundrum supports racism in all of its forms including, but not limited to post-racism, color blindness, and neo-racism, for example. Like most forms of oppression, we may hope that it magically disappears as a result of our good intentions and a little sensitivity training. Yet without intentional recognition, interrogation, radical transformation, or dismantling by all Americans, we fool ourselves into believing that the progress we desire in the areas of equality, equity, justice, and inclusion will have a deep and/or lasting impact. This interdisciplinary volume focuses on the Whiteness Conundrum as it manifests in the form of neo-racism. According to Balibar and Wallerstein (1991), Caballero-Mengibar (2010), and Lee and Rice (2007) neo-racism can be viewed as a transnational phenomenon, and all encompassing "tactical adaptation" that rendered racism more pervasive than in the past by moving beyond targeting groups based on their phenotype and biology alone. Nationality, culture, and identities were now also in play as a means to protect borders and maintain cultural purity among the people. According to Lee and Rice (2007).

> Neo-racism finds refuge in popular understandings of 'human nature' and appeals to the 'common sense' nationalist instincts . . .

Discrimination becomes, seemingly, justified by cultural difference or national origin rather than by 'natural tendencies' to preserve group cultural identity—in this case the dominant group (p. 389).

It is a type of cloaked ethnocentrism according to Barnard-Naudé (2011) as he cites Balibar's "racism without races" concept in an essay on how neo-racism is impacting Europe. Cabellero-Mengibar (2010) uses Spain as an example, and cites how immigrants to that country are rhetorically framed in media as threats to Spanish identity and perceived as the perpetual "them" in comparison to the Spanish "us." Here in the United States, neo-racism's poisonous tentacles still primarily target people of African descent, in addition to anyone perceived as "other," such as immigrants, Native Americans, Muslims, the economically disenfranchised, and members of LGBTQ communities, for example.

Neo-racism according to Balibar (1991) is "A racism which does not have a pseudo-biological concept of race as its main driving force has always existed" (p. 23). In Europe the author spoke of its manifestation in the form of anti-Semitism and the conflation of Arabs and Muslims. Today in the United States neo-racism exploits the intersectionality of our identities in order to further discrimination rather than eradicate it. Under neo-racism, there are few safe spaces for those viewed as "other."

According to Collins (2015), Intersectionality is about ". . . moving beyond a mono-categorical focus on racial inequality to encompass multiple forms of inequality that are organized in a similar logic" (p. 5). Crenshaw (2015), who coined the term intersectionality some 30 years ago as a means of bringing to light the connection of race and gender in Black women's fight for equality, views the term more expansively today to include people of color within LGBTQ movements; girls of color in the fight against the school-to-prison pipeline; women within immigration movements; trans women within feminist movements; and people with disabilities fighting police abuse—all of whom face vulnerabilities that reflect the intersections of racism, sexism, class oppression, transphobia, ableism, and more.

The perspectives covered in this book are presented to expand the ongoing dialogues about Obama's presidency beyond the post-racial fantasy. The nation's festering wound grounded in the Whiteness Conundrum remains in need of treatment. As a result, this book is intended to provide a space for discourses about our intersecting identities and intermingling cultures at this pivotal moment when neo-racism has taken center stage. Contributors examine manifestations of neo-racism from a number of viewpoints including masculinities, leadership, homosexuality, group identity, discriminatory policies, comedic representations, and Creole spaces as they relate to identity. It is divided into two sections that are soft rather than hard divisions. Part I focuses on President Obama while the second part explores the impact of his policies, practices, and presence.

In chapter 1, Zoë Hess Carney examines the rhetorical constraints of the presidency primarily through Obama's inaugural speeches. She writes that the invisible power of Whiteness permeating American culture and society enables and constrains the rhetoric of those who serve as president. Yet, through his speeches, Obama was still able to shift the focus in his addresses beyond tales of the rugged individualistic White American male to include the collectivism of groups that have often been excluded from the mythology of the American dream.

Shanette Harris examines what it means to be Black, male, and President of the United States through her exploration of transformational masculinity. She proposes that transformational masculinity enacted by President Obama made accessible a corresponding transformation in the performance of femininity by Black women as exemplified by First Lady Michelle Obama. In other words, the space created by the President's transformational masculinity meant Mrs. Obama did not have to perform Black womanhood as powerful without superpowers. According to Harris, these gender role norms surpass the bipolar representation of traditional masculine and feminine norms adhered to by European Americans.

Discussing third-space leadership, Omowale Elson asserts that the issue of hybridity (mixed race/trans-ethnicity) became more complex when it reflected a dimension of power that was unavailable to Blacks prior to Obama's meteoric rise to the presidency. In his chapter he juxtaposes Obama's third-space leadership with that of the Black Nationalist movement's leadership arguing that the Black Nationalist's agenda, and their perception of leadership in black-and-white, resulted in their not being able to view Obama's presidency as a new opportunity for progress.

Part II opens with Nura Sediqe's analysis of the hopes and experiences of Muslims during Obama's tenure. While it was anticipated among Muslims that an Obama presidency would relieve some of their pressures as a result of being viewed as the threat within, the opposite in fact turned out to be true. Sediqe shows how policies sustained by the Obama administration resulted in Muslims having to reorganize themselves into an unanticipated collective in response to being discriminated against by an administration headed by a man with a Muslim name, and who himself was perceived by many to be a Muslim.

Co-authors Andrew Spieldenner, Tomeka Robinson, and Anjuliet Woodruffe interrogate the National HIV/AIDS Strategy (NAAS). Though

Obama was the first U.S. president to produce a national strategy, the authors critique its discriminatory representation of certain communities, particularly Black gay men and Black women. The authors view the linking of Blackness to HIV/AIDS as detrimental not only for those populations, but also in terms of how making the connection stymies conversation in Black communities and their organizations.

Jenny Ungbha Korn covers comedy in a serious light, stating that comedians enjoy a self-described liberty in depicting the racial understandings of society through humor. She suggests that comedy about Obama provided timely insight into the construction and fluidity of contemporary meanings of not just "Blackness," but also (surprisingly) the role of "Whiteness" in defining and contextualizing the first Black President of the United States. According to Korn, comedic conceptualizations of Obama responded to racial, cultural, historical, political, economic, and social ideologies of the United States of America and re-articulated the differences between African Americans and Caucasian Americans in creating and perpetuating racialized categories via humor.

In the last chapter, Douglas-Wade Brunton focuses on identity and belonging in the United States beyond the hyphen through the idea of a creolized space. Making comparisons to his home of Trinidad and Tobago, he addresses the belonging of Obama in the U.S. through a processing of creolized territories. He is of the view that recognizing the United States as a Creole space that embodies all who have been here may shift our understanding of who is American.

The aforementioned chapters provide critical analyses of neo-race realities as they pertained to our identities during the Obama era. They show that while the change we desired to believe in may have occurred at some level, the deep and necessary change, namely the racial wound cleansing required to heal, continues to elude us seemingly by design. This book presents some of our ills as manifested in a neo-race reality and assists in our comprehension of what *is* rather than what was *hoped* for as a nation with regard to race.

References

Balibar, E., & Wallerstein, I. (1991). Race, nation, class: Ambiguous identities. London: Verso.

Barnard-Naudé, J. (2011, December 15). "Racism without races." Retrieved from: http://www.thoughtleader.co.za/jacobarnardnaude/2011/12/15/racism-without-races/

Caballero-Mengibar, A. (2010). Neo-racism and the imagination of a Spanish Identity. *Tensoes mundials World Tensions*, 5(8), pp. 89–108.

Collins, P. H. (2015). Intersectionality's definintional dilemmas. *The Annual Review of Sociology* (41), pp. 1–20.
Crenshaw, K. (September 24, 2015). *Why intersectionality can't wait*. Retrieved from https://www.washingtonpost.com/news/in-theory/wp/2015/09/24/why-intersectionality-cant-wait/?utm_term=.fdcd99ce4082
C-Span (2004). Barack Obama Speech at the 2004 DNC Convention. Retrieved from https://search.yahoo.com/yhs/search?p=obama's+speech+at+dnc+2004&ei=UTF-8&hspart=mozilla&hsimpp=yhs-001
Harris, H. E. (2010). The Webbed Message: Re-visioning the American Dream. In H. E. Harris, K. R. Moffitt, & C. R. Squires (Eds.), *The Obama effect: Multidisciplinary renderings of the 2008 campaign* (pp. 65–74). Albany, New York: SUNY Press.
Iton, R. (2008). In search of the black fantastic: Politics and popular culture in the post-civil rights era. New York: Oxford University Press.
Lee, J., & Rice, C. (2007). Welcome to America? International student perceptions of discrimination. *Higher Education*, 53(3), p. 381–409.
Squires, C. (2014). *The post-racial mystique: media and race in the twenty-first century*. New York: New York University Press.

Part I

1
―――

Obama's Transformation of American Myths

Zoë Hess Carney

When Barack Obama was elected, he embodied at least some of the "hope" and "change" that was central to his campaign. As the first Black president in a long line of chief executives, many Americans saw Obama's status as the realization of Martin Luther King's dream and proof that the United States is a "post-racial" society (Hoerl, 2012). However, data show that the U.S. is far from post-racial. For instance, in 2014, only 5.3 percent of Whites were unemployed, while 11.3 percent of African Americans were unemployed, along with the same percentage of American Indians and 10.2 percent of individuals with two or more races (United States Bureau of Labor and Statistics, 2015, p. 6). Pew Research analysts Kochhar and Fry (2014) noted that wealth inequality between Blacks and Whites increased between 2007 and 2014. In 2008, only .14 percent of the White population was incarcerated, while .79 percent of the African-American community and .27 percent of the Hispanic population were in correctional facilities (King & Smith, 2011, p. 277). According to a 2012 United States Sentencing Commission study, Black male offenders' sentences exceeded sentence length for White male offenders by 19.5 percent (p. 108). And, of course, police brutality that spurred the #blacklivesmatter movement also exemplifies a racial divide and institutional racism in the United States These are only a few examples of continued racism in the U.S. since Obama's 2008 election, a reality that Obama addressed throughout his terms.

If certainly not a post-racial society, Obama's presidency could signify what some theorists have called a "neo-racist" society (Balibar, 1991). This chapter explores how Obama has navigated and challenged a neo-racist society (that believes it is post-racial) through his inaugural addresses. Specifically, I show how Obama transformed myths that are historically used to "other," to instead show the "other" as the hero, the pioneer, and the quintessential "good American."

Myths are narratives that express a people's identity, ideology, and moral consciousness through the passing down of stories, eventually abstracted into common metaphors and icons. These abstractions make their appearance as colloquial common sense and serve both to "validate a certain social order" and to instruct future decision-making, actions, and beliefs of a community (Dorsey, 1997, p. 453; Slotkin, 1992, p. 5–6). By tracing how these myths were formed and articulated over time, we can see important narratives of American history—narratives that express national values by locating heroes and villains of the American imagination.

I argue that Obama drew primarily on the myths of the self-made man and the American Dream throughout his campaign speech that led to his first election, and that there was a marked shift in how he used these myths between his campaign speech and his first inaugural address. In his second inaugural address, Obama used the frontier myth as his primary rhetorical resource. In each of these instances, Obama altered the myths' traditional protagonists. Heroes who embody the myth of the self-made man and the frontier myth are similar in character: both rely on the belief that through hard work one can achieve material well-being as "masters of their environment and hence, of their future" (Heale, 1973, p. 412). This sense of agency is revealed as individualism in the self-made man and within the community in the frontier myth. Rhetorically, of course, the two myths overlap, but they have clear divergent rhetorical markers, which Americans may accentuate or mask depending on the story they are telling. Obama's use of the self-made man myth and the American Dream myth united the striving American community, the successful and self-made individual, and race. His use of the frontier myth emphasized progress and collectivism with the purpose of creating justice for the oppressed.

Obama altered historically racist, sexist, and hegemonic myths to highlight a different protagonist, thereby challenging neo-racism. My argument proceeds in four parts. First, I discuss Obama's first-term campaign speeches. In drawing on these myths of the self-made man and the American Dream, Obama positioned himself, a Black American with a multicultural background, as a hero citizen, unsettling what it means to be an American and infusing race into the American story. Second, I discuss a shift in Obama's use of myth in his first inaugural address. Obama focused on collective agency and responsibility instead of praising the character of the individual. Third, I discuss Obama's use of the frontier myth in his second inaugural address. Obama expanded "pioneer" to include historically disenfranchised groups. In this section I explain how Obama's use of the frontier myth successfully challenged neo-racism even though Obama was not as explicit about racial division as some past presidents. This shows the potential of the institution of the presidency to constrain speech on race. It also exhibits how Obama made creative use of the generic mythic elements of the inaugural address to challenge neo-racism despite these constraints. Finally, I discuss the implications of Obama's use of myths, showing how in doing so, Obama empowered those "othered" throughout U.S. history.

Obama as a Self-Made Man with an American Dream

The myth of the self-made man is one of the earliest and longest enduring American myths. It is also referred to that of the "rugged individual" or the "Horatio Alger" myth, named after an author whose stories feature young men who, through hard work and other virtues, become materially successful. I choose to term the narrative "the myth of the self-made man," over more gender-neutral options because gender bias is an important characteristic of the myth itself. The myth implicitly argues that "masculine," physical work makes successful men. It is not a story for women or others who do not fit into a particular cultural conception of what it means to be masculine, nor is it a story for those who are not White, nor is it meant for those unable to become successful. When employed in inaugurals, the myth reduces the "American experience" to the one of the White male and implies that material success is equally available to all.

Benjamin Franklin is perhaps the strongest, and arguably the first, example of an American to write what is now considered the myth of the self-made man (Cawelti, 1965). In his autobiography, Franklin (2006) composed his version of his life—complete with his virtuous character of temperance, silence, order, resolution, frugality, industry, sincerity, justice, moderation, cleanliness, tranquility, chastity, and humility (the last of which is in "imitation of Jesus and Socrates"). Franklin suggested that his personal successes were a direct result of these virtues, and therefore, that anyone who emulated these virtues could also succeed. He argued implicitly for a causal relationship between masculine virtue and success.

Horatio Alger's late-nineteenth-century tales, similar to Franklin's own, "enact a successful struggle to overcome less than spectacular origins and reap justly deserved economic and personal rewards" (Catano, 2001, p. 1). The Horatio Alger myth is the classic rags-to-riches story that teachers pass down to students, and parents to children—the story of upward mobility that says, "You can be anything you want to be if you just try hard enough." Alger most prominently articulated the values of independence and self-reliance above all—if a man worked hard enough, was temperate, saved [his] money, and exercised masculinity in his toiling, he could and would succeed. Success, for the purposes of this myth, means material and social advancement. Likewise, if one proves unsuccessful, it is due to a moral failure, partly because of the myth's assumption of equality. Alger attributed success to effort (and a little bit of luck), and erased the role of privilege.

In the 1920s, the popularity of the Horatio Alger myth declined, and the use of the phrase "American Dream" became popular (Ghosh, 2012, p. 100). Because the American Dream finds its basis in the same narrative as the Horatio Alger myth, it is also raced and gendered. The American Dream "reflects a national self-portrait of Whites," which ignores and erases stories of non-Whites (Dorsey, 2012, p. 150). It also restricts the capacity of other virtues, other definitions of "success," to impinge on the parameters set by these myths. The myth of the self-made man, the Horatio Alger myth, and the American Dream myth overlap, all telling the story of model U.S. citizens—young men who aspire to greatness, work hard, and achieve their dreams.

According to Cloud (1996), a problem within these myths is "tokenism." That is, when media outlets frame successful minorities, they "prove" that the Horatio Alger myth is reality, and that this reality is positive and just. When minorities succeed and are framed as representative of what anyone can do if they just try hard enough, it is difficult to critique problematic social and political structures. The self-made man myth operates with the belief that everyone can succeed no matter his (or her) race, class, or gender, because there is equal opportunity in America. Then, when some Americans are poorer, less educated, and less successful than others, it follows that their outcome is just. If everyone has an equal opportunity, then the only cause for someone's lack of standing is their own "indolence, extravagance, or whatever their 'vices' they might have" (Ghosh, 2012, p. 122). Lack of success is always due to personal moral failure. Despite the inegalitarian outcomes the American Dream promotes, ordinary citizens and politicians continue to employ the American Dream because the heroic, self-made figure that it produces powerfully resonates in American culture—the individual *ethos* of success has the power to move the American audience (Murphy, 2003).

Obama's use of the American Dream myth, though, did not tokenize Obama as a "model minority" who pulled himself up by his bootstraps because, as Dorsey (2012) argued, Obama infused race into the story instead of sidelining it. Obama (2006) mentioned the American Dream in his book *The Audacity of Hope*, writing that the American story is "the story of farmers and soldiers, in Kansas and Kenya, on the shores of Hawaii and in the streets of Chicago. It's a varied and unlikely journey, but one that's held together by the same simple dream. And that is why it's an American story" (p. 242). Instead, Obama positioned multi-culturalism and multi-racialism as central to the American story, and in doing so, he revealed a new kind of self-made man.[1] For instance, Obama placed himself as part of Reverend Martin Luther King Jr.'s trajectory, identifying himself as part of the "Joshua Generation" in his 2007 address in Selma, Alabama, and in a 2008 address commemorating the fortieth anniversary of King's death (Darsey, 2009, pp. 25–26; Dorsey, 2012; Murphy, 2011). In these instances, Obama included race in the self-made American man's story.

Obama made a similar rhetorical move when Trayvon Martin, an unarmed Black teenager, was shot and killed by George Zimmerman, a neighborhood watch coordinator. Obama responded with a statement explicitly about race, saying, "My main message is to the parents of Trayvon Martin. If I had a son, he'd look like Trayvon. I think they are right to expect that all of us as Americans are going to take this with the seriousness it deserves" (Shear, 2013). In a later statement, Obama expounded on that line, saying that not only could Martin "have been my son," Martin "could have been me 35 years ago." He used his personal identification with Martin and Martin's parents to bring recognition to the "set of experiences and a history" from which the African-American community experienced Martin's violent death (The White House, United States Government, 2013). That is, Obama reflected on systemic racism against Blacks in America. In these instances, Obama brought to the fore particularly African-American experiences, placing himself within this communal history, and drawing attention to problematic racial issues in contemporary America.

Two years later, following another instance of racial violence against Blacks, Obama delivered a eulogy for Clementa Pinckney. Pinckney was a South Carolina Senator assassinated at Emanuel African Methodist Episcopal Church in Charleston, where he served as senior pastor. In addition to speaking about the life and legacy of Pinckney, Obama once again explained historical and systemic racial injustice. He said,

> Maybe we now realize the way racial bias can infect us even when we don't realize it, so that we're guarding against not just racial slurs, but we're also guarding against the subtle impulse

to call Johnny back for a job interview but not Jamal. So that we search our hearts when we consider laws to make it harder for some of our fellow citizens to vote. By recognizing our common humanity by treating every child as important, regardless of the color of their skin or the station into which they were born, and to do what's necessary to make opportunity real for every American—by doing that, we express God's grace. (The White House, United States Government, 2015)

Here, Obama connected the death of Pinckney with a larger problem of racism in the United States. Obama also sang "Amazing Grace," and he did so "distinctly in the style of the Black church" (Manseau, 2015). In doing so, Obama performed Black culture and spoke about Black struggle, showing that Blacks are harmed in the U.S. every day because of racism. Only by rectifying these practices may Americans show God's grace.

In addition to identifying with African Americans at moments of tragedy, Obama interjected a story of upward mobility for people who have diverse backgrounds—for him, a childhood moving between Hawaii and Indonesia, without his father, and sometimes without his mother—as part of the American story. This story depicted a reality in which citizens have complete power to carve out their own success: in doing so, he represented all Americans as having agency, not in spite of their race, but sometimes because of it. He endorsed variation as part of the American experience while retaining the exceptional status of the protagonist who achieves his goals.

Obama's message had the potential to empower those whose stories are usually erased in the American story by acknowledging race and positioning his own individuality as "reflective of the strength common to the rugged individual"—highlighting American mythic commonality between Blacks and Whites, while marking Blackness as being a part of the American myth (Dorsey, 2012, p. 151). Obama's portrayal of himself as a self-made man served to unify Black and White Americans, positioning a particular American *ethos* as the most important element to a person's success. He reinforced the idea that Americans are strong and independent, and while doing so, highlighted race as an important aspect of the American narrative, which confronts a discourse of White hegemonic national identity.

Obama employed the myth of the self-made man in pursuit of the American Dream in a way that incorporated his race into the American story. Obama altered the myth of the self-made man and the American Dream in a different way in his inaugural address, fitting within the constraints of the genre while continuing to confront neo-racism.

Obama's Inaugural Addresses

Obama's two inaugural addresses challenged neo-racism in different ways, though both invoked national myths. The first inaugural address drew upon the value of hard work found in the myth of the self-made man and the American Dream. Obama's hero-citizen in this narrative, though, was not one who acted alone—instead he worked with, and on behalf of, others. Thus, the first inaugural address shows how Obama altered a national myth to create impetus for collective social action. The second inaugural address takes more liberty with a national myth. In this speech, Obama continued the theme of valuing collective action while expanding the type of hero central to the narrative. Obama's hero in his second inaugural is a person historically "othered" in the U.S., be that because of race, gender, sexuality, age, or citizenship status.

Inaugural addresses are epideictic speech—that is, they are ceremonial, they focus on the present, and they work symbolically. In enacting the inaugural address, the president "unifies the audience by reconstituting 'the people,' rehearses communal values drawn from the past, sets forth the political principles that will guide the new administration, and demonstrates through enactment that the president appreciates the requirements and limitations of the executive office" (Campbell & Jamieson, 2008, pp. 31–32). In inaugural addresses, presidents draw upon *memoria*, or a shared past to remind the people of the most important national values that define the people and that will anchor the actions of his presidential term. Because inaugural addresses draw upon a collective memory, presidents often draw upon national myths for their rhetorical invention (Beasley, 2001; Frank, 2011; Fulmer, 1986). Obama is no exception to this norm, though he altered traditional myths, thereby challenging neo-racism.

Obama's inaugural addresses show how a president can draw upon myths to fight inequality. In this way, the myths offer a way for Obama to code his anti-racist speech in a way that White presidents do not. Given Obama's practice of speaking about race throughout his presidency, and because race is particularly salient for Obama, Obama's indirect challenge of neo-racism shows one constraint of race on presidential speech—Obama would presumably receive backlash if he spoke directly about anti-Black racism in an inaugural address.

There are several instances of White presidents speaking about racial issues, and specifically those concerning African Americans, in inaugural addresses. As Wilson (2005) noted, President James Garfield spent nearly half of his 1881 inaugural address on the issue of African Americans being denied voting rights, and Grover Cleveland pled for African Americans to receive the legal equality they are granted by the Constitution in his 1885 inaugural address (pp. 23–24). Garfield (1881) said in his inaugural address that to "violate the freedom and sanctities of the suffrage is more than an evil. It is a crime which, if persisted in, will destroy the Government itself." No small threat, Garfield presented the end of the government as the consequence of denying African Americans the vote. Likewise, Grover Cleveland (1885) said in his inaugural address that "[i]n the administration of a government pledged to do equal and exact justice to all men there should be no pretext for anxiety touching the protection of the freedmen in their [African Americans'] rights or their security in the enjoyment of their privileges under the Constitution and its amendments." For Cleveland, to even discuss that African Americans should not be afforded the same rights and obligations as all other citizens "is idle and unprofitable." Benjamin Harrison (1889), too, spoke of the benefits of the right to the ballot being open to all without distinction of race in his inaugural address. In all of these instances, the inaugural rhetoric of White presidents bound racial inequality of Black Americans with national problems of the United States as a whole.

A helpful case for understanding how inaugural addresses enable White presidents to speak about race is found in Bill Clinton's presidency. Clinton referred to the nation's racial divide as "America's constant curse" in his 1997 inaugural address. Moreover, Clinton (1997) placed himself within the African-American experience when he used his inaugural address to echo Lyndon B. Johnson, saying, "We shall overcome [this divide]." "We Shall Overcome" originated as an anthem in the civil rights movement and later in the words of Martin Luther King Jr., Parry-Giles & Parry-Giles (2006) noted that for most of U.S. history, White identity "has been the basis for a series of exclusionary policies and the overall cultural and political hegemony of the community" (p. 87). By using the words "we shall overcome" in an inaugural address, Clinton situated himself—and thus, the rest of the nation—into the Black experience, making it the "American experience." In Clinton's rhetoric, a hegemonic culture of Whiteness that once excluded African Americans now recognizes them. Moreover, when Clinton used "We shall overcome," Black Americans—for a moment—actually became the central identifier and agent of what it means to be American.

Johnson and Clinton were able to briefly centralize Black Americans within the hegemonic White-American identity, at least in part because they are White. It is safe to imagine the empowerment of non-Whites when the "Leader of the Free World," a White president, created that fiction. While Clinton's association with African Americans was superficial, making the use of "we" in "we shall overcome," safe and impersonal, separating Clinton from the African-American experience, Obama embodies this experience. The institutional norm of Whiteness enables White presidents to speak about racial issues on behalf of the nation in inaugural addresses. Conversely, Whiteness constrains the rhetoric of Black presidents, thus limiting their capacity to enact racial change, even from the nation's most powerful political office. Obama creatively maneuvered around this constraint by drawing on language and familiar structure of American myths while altering these myths to talk about race. Moreover, he invoked explicit reflections on race in speeches other than his inaugural addresses.

Obama's First Inaugural

Obama was elected in 2008 after campaigning on the ideas of "hope" and "change." He began presiding during "the country's most severe financial crisis since the Great Depression" and into the role of Commander in Chief of a country amidst two wars (Frank, 2011, p. 619). These three pieces of context: running on progress after Bush, being placed within the burden of an economic crisis, and leading a country in two wars, help us understand the rhetoric of his first inaugural address, given on January 20, 2009, to a crowd of approximately 1.8 million people—the largest in-person inaugural address audience in history ("How Many Attended," 2013).

Cyril Ghosh (2012) noted that in periods of transformation, in crisis, when "real wages erode," politicians cling to ideologies to claim legitimacy, which are, in this case, imbedded in myths. During the Great Depression, signature Horatio Alger phrases such as "bootstrapping" and "struggling manfully in adversity pays off materially" appeared in the American vocabulary (p. 100). If comparing the rhetorical situation of the two—the Great Depression and the Great Recession of 2008—it would make sense for Obama to rely on the rugged individual when describing hero-citizens in his inaugural. This rugged individual, according to Troy Murphy (2003) usually "emphasizes individual acts largely divorced from the arena of politics and marked by quiet humility as a distinct antidote to public advocacy" (p. 203).

Past presidential speeches show this characterization of the model citizen. President Reagan's heroes were the ones whose patriotism ran "quiet but deep" and President Nixon's were those of the "silent majority." President Bush told stories about individuals—self-made and Horatio Alger-like—whom he called post-9-11 "heroes." These heroes, if they wanted to "fight terrorism," could become a "September 11th volunteer" by such activities as mentoring a child or comforting the afflicted—none of which are political or particularly active (Murphy, 2003, pp. 200–205).

Obama's inaugural address hero-citizens, by contrast, were hard workers, not quiet or humble. Instead, they were people who were never "settling for less." They were the "risk-takers, the doers, the makers of things" ("Barack Obama's Inaugural Address," 2009). In describing heroes as "risk-takers" who were never satisfied, Obama implied that changes within the system needed to be made, a point he articulated more explicitly in his second inaugural than in his first.

The second change Obama made to the heroic citizenship narratives (like the self-made man and the American Dream) was to nuance individualism with strength in the collective. The historical myths emphasize citizens "acting alone, often spontaneously, and generally without the assistance or support of a larger community structure" (Murphy, 2003, p. 203). Many presidents rely on these individual-praising myths, especially if they are conservative. Rowland and Jones (2007) argued that the value of individualism found in the American Dream has, for the past twenty years, been tied to conservatism; thus, the power of the narrative has helped the Republican Party pass conservative policies. Rowland and Jones (2007) noted that in Obama's Democratic Convention keynote address in 2004, Obama offered a vision for America that is nuanced with individualism and collective responsibility, tilting the narrative in favor of liberal policies. Obama continued using this nuanced narrative that values collective responsibility in his inaugural when he said, "For us, they packed up their few worldly possessions and traveled across oceans in search of a new life. For us, they toiled in sweatshops and settled the West; endured the lash of the whip and plowed the hard earth. For us, they fought and died, in places like Concord and Gettysburg; Normandy and Khe Sanh" ("Barack Obama's Inaugural Address," 2009). The heroes Obama mentioned are immigrants, workers, pioneers, and soldiers. They were, according to Obama, people who worked for the good of the whole nation. Obama's heroes were those who "saw America as bigger than the sum of our individual ambitions, greater than all the differences of birth or wealth or faction" ("Barack Obama's Inaugural Address," 2009). In this section, Obama called out those who have been othered by neo-racism and puts them in the place of the traditionally White pioneer.

In books and other pre-presidential discourse, Obama relied on the myth of the self-made man through the telling of the American Dream. He was the representative model character in these campaign discourses—a Black man, who, through hard work, succeeded even within the confines of a still racist America. But he did not employ this narrative in his inaugural address. He shifted to a story that favored collective action, and when he did mention the individual, the individuals were change-makers, not "ordinary citizens."

This shift can be partially attributed to the different speech genres. The purpose of campaign rhetoric is to bolster the speaker. Inaugural addresses are, instead, meant to reflect America's story. These speeches unite the nation, celebrate a transfer of power, shed light on the past, explain the present, and give vision for the future. When Obama told America's story in his inaugural, he tweaked the narrative of the self-made man to value collective responsibility. This was a natural transition into his version of the frontier myth, which characterized his second inaugural.

Obama's Second Inaugural

By the time of Obama's second inaugural address, the United States was technically only engaged in one war, but Obama was still facing many challenges: congressional budget issues, a lowering, but still high, unemployment rate, and discord about gun control and immigration. Obama delivered his address on Martin Luther King Day, January 21, 2013, to a crowd of approximately one million people. The speech focused on action, and was more partisan than is typical of the genre, as he spoke about "liberal issues" such as gay rights and climate change ("How Many Attended," 2013).

In Obama's second inaugural address, he needed to unify the audience, rehearse communal values, set forth political principles, and demonstrate a respect for the requirements and constraints of the office, which are all requirements of the inaugural address genre (Campbell & Jamieson, 1990, 2008). He also had to show that the country could, indeed, move "forward" under a second term of his presidency. Obama used an old American narrative, the frontier myth, and transformed it to fit his vision for the United States. Obama, empowered by being elected to a second term, appropriated the old frontier myth to tell a different American story, one that recognized and expanded the rights of others.

The story of American progress, expansion, and originally, the conquering of the west, characterizes the frontier myth (Turner, 1983). This myth, which Richard Slotkin argued is "our oldest and most characteristic myth, expressed in a body of literature, folklore, ritual, historiography, and polemics produced over a period of three centuries," is similar to the self-made man myth, but it places a higher value on sacrifice for the sake of helping the community progress (Slotkin, 1992, p. 10). The myth tells the story of White American settlers who valued civilization, community, and democracy, moving west, triumphing over "savage" American Indians, and taming the frontier (Slotkin, 1992; Stuckey, 2011). It explains the establishment of American colonies, and it accounts for America's emergence as a nation-state, its economic growth, and its process of modernization (Slotkin, 1992). The frontier myth is the narrative of the United States.

The frontier myth is also historically raced, usually focusing on the success of White men. Moreover, the success of Whites is understood in the frontier myth to be of divine origin. For example, Stuckey (2004) explained that because of the "cultural fiction of White superiority" that characterized American life during the time of westward expansion, when the frontier myth was conceived, American Indians were both "rendered invisible" and "understood as doomed." This understanding of the value and fate of American Indians was tied to the belief that their doom, and the success of White settlers, was the will of God (pp. 45–47). Manifest Destiny, and the idea of God's will demanding that White men will conquer and defeat "savages," seems archaic. However, this belief did not die out during the era of western expansion. Nativists in the early twentieth century used the trope of "savage groups" to imagine immigrants and Blacks. Moreover, racial violence such as lynching and race riots "routinely invoked the mythic language of Armageddon" (Dorsey, 2007, p. 42). In this narrative, it is not immoral for Whites to be self-interested at the expense of others, and non-Whites can do nothing about the matter.

In his second inaugural, Obama invoked the frontier myth, but changed its protagonist. Obama told a story of the American people as pioneers who must work together to gain equality for all citizens, and only in this way were they truly American. Stuckey (2004) explained that pioneers, the heroes of the frontier myth, are understood "as heroic, self-sacrificing, brave, and enduring," and that we valorize these characteristics when we use the myth to understand our national identity (p. 251). Obama's hero citizen was a part of a collective citizenship with these pioneer characteristics. These citizens had one goal, one mark to reach, and that was to make equality a reality.

Obama presented the principal goal of equality by appealing to the Declaration of Independence—America's original radical claim to independence and equality. The Declaration of Independence, which framed the argument of equality, is not a conservative document. It was written, and is employed, for the purpose of invoking change. Obama's use of the Declaration of Independence illuminates a key mythic element of his speech: Americans were once again pioneers, not self-made men, who were exceptional because of their allegiance to equality. Obama said:

> We recall that what binds this nation together is not the colors of our skin or the tenants of our faith or the origins of our names. What makes us exceptional—what makes us American—is our allegiance to an idea, articulated in a declaration made more than two centuries ago: 'We hold these truths to be self-evident, that all men are created equal, that they are endowed by their Creator with certain unalienable rights, that among these are Life, Liberty, and the pursuit of Happiness.' ("Inaugural Address," 2013)

Explained in this way, the very reason there is a community of people who act as citizens of the United States was because of their commitment to the idea that people are created equal. Obama set a path for citizen heroes from the very beginning. If the reason for existence is an adherence to an idea, then the one path to follow is to make that idea come to fruition.

That these pioneers must change the system in order to bring about true equality marks the second locus worthy of investigation in Obama's frontier myth. Obama's pioneers have agency. For Obama, "All men who are created equal" is active, not passive. To be realized, it requires conscious action on behalf of citizens; it is not part of God's divine plan, destined to be true without human involvement. Obama said, "these truths may be self-evident," but "they have never been self-executing," meaning that Americans must take it upon themselves to "carry into an uncertain future that precious light of freedom." All Americans must work toward the goal of equality. This differs from the traditional pioneer myth in which Whites conquer all because it is God's will.

Obama continued the theme of collective action on behalf of racial equality when he alluded to two of Lincoln's speeches on slavery. He said: "through blood drawn by lash, and blood drawn by sword, we learned that no union founded on the principles of liberty and equality could survive half-slave and half-free. We made ourselves anew, and vowed to move forward together" ("Inaugural Address," 2013). Here Obama referenced the racial divide without speaking directly about the institutional racism that has existed in the United States since chattel slavery. By echoing past presidents and by using collective language, Obama challenged continued racism in the U.S. He placed America's success on whether or not the citizens would unify and seek justice.

Obama's pioneers were those who sought justice for Black Americans, women, and the gay community. He said equality was the star that "guided our forebears through Seneca Falls, and Selma, and Stonewall, just as it guided all those men and women, sung and unsung, who left footprints along this great Mall, to hear a preacher say that we cannot walk alone, to hear a King proclaim that our individual freedom is inextricably bound to the freedom of every soul on Earth" ("Inaugural Address," 2013). In this section, Obama recognized and challenged neo-racism and oppression of gender and sexuality. He changed the "pioneer"—usually a masculine, White American—into Black Americans, women, members of the LGBTQ community, and their allies.

Obama continued widening the definition of the American pioneer to include immigrants and children. Obama said:

> Our journey is not complete until our gay brothers and sisters are treated like anyone else under the law . . . until no citizen is forced to wait for hours to exercise the right to vote. . . . until we find a better way to welcome the striving, hopeful immigrants who still see America as a land of opportunity . . . until bright young students and engineers are enlisted in our workforce rather than expelled from our country . . . until all our children, from the streets of Detroit to the hills of Appalachia, to the quiet lanes of Newtown, know that they are cared for and cherished and always safe from harm. ("Inaugural Address," 2013)

In this section, Obama not only included groups of people usually excluded from the frontier myth, he also hinted at specific policy goals, such as gay marriage, voting reform, and gun control. While inaugurals usually amplify or rehearse admitted facts, Obama employed a national myth to expand the rights and agency of people who have been othered in America, both culturally and institutionally, presenting unrealized rights as a natural part of the American story and *ethos*.

For example, by placing gay marriage in the list of inherent equalities given by God, Obama implicitly argued that gay marriage is a natural right that can be found in the Declaration of Independence. He presented a version of reality in which gay rights are necessary for the United States to fulfill its role as an exceptional country. After all, pioneers are innately characterized by their "allegiance to an idea" of equality ("Inaugural Address," 2013). By placing the presumption of gay rights as essential to equality, Obama inferred that American citizens must recognize gay marriage in order to fulfill their role as exceptional pioneers bound to equality as a marker of identity. This is reminiscent of Obama's first inaugural address, in which he said that the source of "our confidence" is the knowledge that "God calls on us to shape an uncertain destiny" ("Barack Obama's Inaugural Address," 2009). Likewise, Obama suggested that if the U.S. is to continue following the guiding star of equality, there is a need for new immigration policies, gun laws, and increased voting rights.

The frontier myth is drenched in exclusionary principles. Obama picked up the myth for his second inaugural address, retaining the theme of progress, expansion, and sacrifice—and inverting the erasure of non-White male citizens. His pioneers must journey until they "make these words, these rights, these values—of life, liberty, and the pursuit of happiness—real for every American" ("Inaugural Address," 2013). Like many presidents, he constituted the people as "pioneers," and these pioneers are concerned, like those of early America, with expansion. In some ways the goal of Obama's modern pioneers were antithetical to the frontier myth, which originally featured conquering American Indians and was also used by Southerners to oppress African Americans and by northern Progressives "to limit the role of immigrants in politics and to halt, or radically restrict, immigration by people of 'inferior' racial stock" (Slotkin, 1992, p. 189). In this narrative, Obama highlighted immigrants and said that the United States must find a better way to welcome them. He claimed that women, immigrants, and the LGBTQ community, likewise, do not enjoy true equality.

In recognizing these inequalities, Obama provided space to critique the system. In his narrative, citizens have agency—God may have given Americans rights, but citizens must work to keep them. He highlighted the hardships of women, the LGBTQ community, and immigrants. Obama did not talk about race explicitly in his State of the Union addresses, which shows constraints on his speech, but he did challenge racism and neo-racism by transforming the frontier myth into one that recognizes the "other" as an American hero and alluding to a history of racist institutions.

Conclusion

Obama's presidency cannot offer rhetorical scholars definitive answers to questions of whether, and how, Black presidents may alter the presidency (Watts, 2010). His presidency can, however, as Mary Stuckey (2010) argued, offer critical leverage to better understand the racial construction of the presidency. That is, through analyzing Obama's discourse, we can begin to understand how race might enable and constrain presidential speech. Thus, this chapter focused on how Obama transformed national myths throughout his presidency in the service of challenging neo-racism. Obama did so by infusing race into his personal story, while using the structure and language of the self-made man and the American Dream in his campaign speeches and first inaugural address. Then, in his second inaugural address, Obama employed the frontier myth, transforming White pioneer protagonists into groups of citizens whose goal is to achieve equality among all citizens.

The American Dream makes "one crucial assumption—everyone can participate equally and can always start over" (Ghosh, 2012, p. 104). Historically, not every American citizen can in fact do so. And when Obama delivered his inaugural speeches, amidst economic strain, resources were scarce and racial and gender inequalities vast. Obama successfully highlighted some of those excluded from the American Dream, and called upon American citizens-as-pioneers to make appropriate changes. Obama challenged neo-racism by drawing upon and transforming racist myths that guide the American people in his inaugural addresses, a genre of speech framed in transcendent national values (Beasley, 2011, p. 10).

Obama used his inaugural addresses to highlight heroes ignored in American national myths. In doing so, he altered what it means to be American. Still, these speeches were constrained by normative Whiteness. Obama used other speech situations to directly lecture on racial injustice, using his *ethos* to identify himself, and thus the American people, with the Black experience. Obama creatively and uniquely challenged neo-racism through public discourse.

References

Balibar, E. (1991). Is there a "Neo-Racism"? In E. Balibar & I. M. Wallerstein, *Race, nation, class: Ambiguous identities* (London: Verso).

Barack Obama's Inaugural Address. (2009, January 20). Retrieved from http://www.nytimes.com/2009/01/20/us/politics/20text-obama.html?pagewanted=all

Beasley, V. B. (2001). The rhetoric of ideological consensus in the United States: American principles and American pose in presidential inaugurals. *Communication Monographs*, 68(2), 169–183.

Beasley, V. B. (2011). *You, the people: American national identity in presidential rhetoric*. College Station: Texas A&M University Press.

Campbell, K. K., & Jamieson, K. H. (1990). *Deeds done in words: Presidential rhetoric and the genres of governance*. Chicago: University of Chicago Press.

Campbell, K. K., & Jamieson, K. H. (2008). *Presidents creating the presidency: Deeds done in words*. Chicago: University of Chicago Press.

Catano, J. V. (2001). *Ragged Dicks: Masculinity, steel, and the rhetoric of the self-made man*. Carbondale, IL: Southern Illinois University Press.

Cawelti, J. G. (1965). *Apostles of the self-made man*. Chicago: University of Chicago Press.
Cleveland, G. (1885, March 4). Inaugural Address. The American Presidency Project. Retrieved from http://www.presidency.ucsb.edu/ws/?pid=25824
Clinton, W. J. (1997, January 20). Inaugural Address. The American Presidency Project. Retrieved from http://www.presidency.ucsb.edu/ws/?pid=54183
Cloud, D. L. (1996). Hegemony or concordance? The rhetoric of tokenism in "Oprah" Oprah rags-to-riches biography. *Critical Studies in Media Communication, 13*(2), 115–137.
Darsey, J. (2009). Barack Obama and America's journey. *Southern Communication Journal, 74*(1), 88–103.
Dorsey, L. G. (1997). Sailing into the "wondrous now": The myth of the American Navy's world cruise. *Quarterly Journal of Speech, 83*(4), 447–465.
Dorsey, L. G. (2012). Narrating the presidential 'race.' Barack Obama and the American dream. In R. L. Jackson II & J. E. Moshin (Eds.), *Communicating marginalized masculinities: Identity politics in TV, film, and new media* (pp. 144–158). Florence, KY: Routledge.
Frank, D. A. (2011). Obama's rhetorical signature: Cosmopolitan civil religion in the presidential inaugural address, January 20, 2009. *Rhetoric & Public Affairs, 14*(4), 605–630.
Franklin, B. (1916). *Autobiography of Benjamin Franklin*. E. Boyd Smith (Ed.). New York: Henry Holt and Company.
Franklin, B. (2006). Project Gutenberg's autobiography of Benjamin Franklin. F. W. Pine (Ed.). Retrieved from https://www.gutenberg.org/files/20203/20203.txt
Fulmer, H. W. (1986). A rhetoric of oldspeak: Mythic elements in presidential inaugural addresses, 1960–1980. *Rhetoric Society Quarterly, 16*(4), 299–312.
Garfield, J. A. (1881, March 4). Inaugural Address. [Transcript.] The American Presidency Project. Retrieved from http://www.presidency.ucsb.edu/ws/?pid=25823
Ghosh, C. (2012). *The Politics of the American dream: Democratic inclusion in contemporary American political culture*. Gordonsville, VA: Palgrave Macmillan.
Harrison, B. (1889, March 4). Inaugural Address. *The American Presidency Project*. Retrieved from http://www.presidency.ucsb.edu/ws/?pid=25825
Heale, M. J. (1973). The role of the frontier in Jacksonian politics: David Crockett and the myth of the self-made man. *The Western Historical Quarterly, 4*(4), 405–423.
Hoerl, K. (2012). Selective amnesia and racial transcendence in news coverage of President Obama's inauguration. *Quarterly Journal of Speech, 98*(2), 178–202.
How many attended Obama's second inauguration? (2013, January 21). Retrieved from http://www.cbsnews.com/news/how-many-attended-obamas-second-inauguration/
Inaugural Address by President Barack Obama (2013, January 21). *The New York Times*. Retrieved from http://www.whitehouse.gov/the-press-office/2013/01/21/inaugural-address-president-barack-obama

King, D. S., & Smith, R. M. (2011). *Still a house divided: Race and politics in Obama's America*. Princeton: Princeton University Press.

Kochhar, R., & Fry, R. (2014, December 12). Wealth inequality has widened along racial, ethnic lines since end of Great Recession. *Pew Research Center*. Retrieved from http://www.pewresearch.org/fact-tank/2014/12/12/racial-wealth-gaps-great-recession/

Manseau, P. (2015, June 30). Obama's graceful pause in Charleston. *The Atlantic*. Retrieved from http://www.theatlantic.com/politics/archive/2015/06/obamas-graceful-pause-in-charleston/397223/

Murphy, J. M. (2011). Barack Obama, the Exodus tradition, and the Joshua generation. *Quarterly Journal of Speech*, 97(4), 387–410.

Murphy, T. A. (2003). Romantic democracy and the rhetoric of heroic citizenship. *Communication Quarterly*, 51(2), 192–208.

Obama, B. (2006). *The audacity of hope: Thoughts on reclaiming the American dream*. New York: Three Rivers Press.

Parry-Giles, T., & Parry-Giles, S. J. (2006). *The prime-time presidency: The West Wing and US nationalism*. Champaign, IL: University of Illinois Press.

Rowland, R. C., & Jones, J. M. (2007). Recasting the American dream and American politics: Barack Obama's keynote address to the 2004 Democratic National Convention. *Quarterly Journal of Speech*, 93(4), 425–448.

Rowland, R. C., & Jones, J. M. (2011). One dream: Barack Obama, race, and the American dream. *Rhetoric & Public Affairs*, 14(1), 125–154.

Shear, M. (2013, March 23). Obama speaks out on Trayvon Martin killing. *New York Times*. Retrieved from http://thecaucus.blogs.nytimes.com/2012/03/23/obama-makes-first-comments-on-trayvon-martin-shooting/

Slotkin, R. (1992). *Gunfighter nation: The myth of the in twentieth-century America*. Norman, OK: University of Oklahoma Press.

Stuckey, M. E. (2004). *Defining Americans: The presidency and national identity*. Lawrence: University Press of Kansas.

Stuckey, M. E. (2010). Rethinking the rhetorical presidency and presidential rhetoric. *Review of Communication*, 10(1), 38–52.

Stuckey, M. E. (2011). The Donner Party and the rhetoric of westward expansion. *Rhetoric & Public Affairs*, 14(2), 229–260.

The White House, United States Government (2013). Remarks by the president on Trayvon Martin. Retrieved from https://www.whitehouse.gov/the-press-office/2013/07/19/remarks-president-trayvon-martin

The White House, United States Government (2015). Remarks by the president in eulogy for the honorable reverend Clementa Pinckney. Retrieved from https://www.whitehouse.gov/the-press-office/2015/06/26/remarks-president-eulogy-honorable-reverend-clementa-Pinckney

Turner, F. J. (1983). The significance of the frontier in American history. In R. H. Carpenter (Ed.), *The eloquence of Frederick Jackson Turner*. San Marcos, CA: The Huntington Library.

United States Bureau of Labor and Statistics (2015). Labor force characteristics by race and ethnicity, 2014. Retrieved from https://www.bls.gov/opub/reports/race-and-ethnicity/archive/labor-force-characteristics-by-race-and-ethnicity-2014.pdf

United States Sentencing Commission (2012). Report on the continuing impact of *United States v. Booker* on Federal Sentencing. Retrieved at http://www.ussc.gov/sites/default/files/pdf/news/congressional-testimony-and-reports/booker-reports/2012-booker/Part_A.pdf#page=55

Watts, E. K. (2010). The problem of race in public address research: W. E. B. Du Bois and the conflicted aesthetics of race. In S. J. Parry-Giles & J. M. Hogan (Eds.), *The handbook of rhetoric and public address* (pp. 373–397). Malden, MA: Wiley-Blackwell.

Wilson, K. H. (2005). The politics of place and presidential rhetoric in the United States, 1875–1901. In J. A. Aune & E. D. Rigsby (Eds.), *Civil Rights rhetoric and the American presidency* (pp. 16–40). College Station: Texas A&M University Press.

2

Transformational Masculinity and Fathering in the Age of Obama

"Roses and Thorns"

Shanette Harris

As Lincoln organized the forces arrayed against slavery he was heard to say: "Of strange, discordant, and even hostile elements, we gathered from the four winds, and formed and fought to battle through." That is our purpose here today. That is why I'm in this race. Not just to hold an office but to gather with you to transform a nation.

—Morgan, 2007, February 10, p. 3

As the first Black family in the White House, the Obamas' image as the quintessential all-American family is all the more remarkable perhaps offering a glimpse of the transformative power of his presidency for reflecting back to us who we are as Americans and who we want to be.

—Michaux, 2013, p. 250

Michelle Obama, wife of the 44th President described varied activities, events, and interactions that occurred during their family's adjustment to White House interviewers. In particular, she used the phrase *"roses and thorns"* to refer to a communication practice that required each family member to share a good *and* bad experience from their day with others at the dinner table. This tradition evolved to make sure that each person could share personal information with family members; although if necessary, all had access to the president at points during the day for important discussions. After Barack Hussein Obama's two-term election as the 44th President of the United States and the first president of African descent, he and his family (i.e., First Lady Michelle Obama, Malia, and Sasha) were critiqued on a regular and repetitive basis and in a more in-depth way than any previous president and First Family. Experiences of the Obama family consistent with their dinner custom of *"roses and thorns"* included a litany of both favorable and challenging circumstances throughout both terms of his presidency.

In 2008 Barack Obama's election as the 44th American President allegedly ushered in a new phase in American history of the twenty-first century of postmodern, post-Civil Rights culture that was imagined to rectify some of the social conditions or "thorns" identified in the African-American community. The overwhelming social history of oppression, discrimination, and marginalization of African Americans contributed to rather high expectations and even magical thinking about the impact this momentous event might have on the lives of those who shared a similar physiognomy (if not cultural heritage) with the President (Hoston, 2014). These citizens believed that a president of African descent would alleviate social ills that had disproportionately affected them for centuries. Others of the same race but different ethnicities who had immigrated to America but previously witnessed leaders of African descent who were elected to office but later proven to be untrustworthy were less enthusiastic (Hartmann, 2008). Still, a minority of African heritage Americans was skeptical, if not suspicious, and questioned the president's race loyalty because of a cultural socialization that differed from the majority of African Americans. However these observers failed to consider the impact of the complexity of covert racism and bias toward a male president of African heritage who "inherited a deflating economy teetering on an outright depression, a skyrocketing debt, the structural legacy of thirty years of politically engineered inequality and two wars." (Dorrien, 2012, p. 7).

This chapter presents a gendered role explanation of the 44th President's terms in office from a social constructionist perspective. A discussion of how masculinity intersects with narratives of race and gender is offered with an emphasis on the value of his election for fathering and African-American males and families. It is proposed that a transformational masculinity enacted by the 44th President also produced uneasiness in European Americans because of challenges to historical stereotypes of

African Americans and threats to hegemonic masculinity associated with traditionalists' fear of loss of privilege. How masculinity interacted with race/ethnicity to influence perceptions of his presidency and transformed narratives of father, husband, and leader are examined.

The 44th President's performance was more highly approved of near the end rather than earlier in his second term, but evidence shows that Americans maintained a mixed view of his leadership with those considered "Millennials" more than twice as likely than "Baby Boomers" to report increases in opportunities and non-Whites more likely than Whites to believe that opportunities increased because of his agenda (52% versus 17%) (Brownstein, 2015). Polarized reactions to the leadership and decision making of the Democratic president of African descent were partly shaped by perceptions that originated in the enslavement of Africans as property or chattel.

Gender Role Narratives and African Americans

Stereotyped exaggerations of Africans that contributed to their initial enslavement underlie contemporary stereotypical social constructions of African Americans. In spite of commonalities in oppression, people of African descent forcibly brought to America were objectified according to gender. The behavioral expectations for slave women and men were substantially more similar than for their European heritage male and female owners. However the greatest achievements as perceived through the eyes of slave owners despite a myriad of domestic and field responsibilities were the conception and birth of offspring. Ultimately it was the contribution of healthy children that translated into more slaves, which in turn, led to greater financial profit for the masters that was seen as beneficial. Forced participation in physical tasks assigned to male slaves and the receipt of similar harsh treatment and abuse during an era that characterized females as weak, passive, and inferior to men but dependent upon their protection and economic provisions, produced a unique and distinct experience for Black women. The combination of domestic responsibilities, participation in male-type work and mandatory reproduction constructed a womanhood that involved expressive and instrumental gender role attitudes and behaviors rather than rigid adherence to a European American feminine gender role orientation (Binion, 1990; Buckley & Carter, 2005).

African-American women were characterized as animals, beasts—mules of the earth who were engaged in excessive labor from dawn to dusk, longsuffering without the support of a man, male protector, or affection

(Collins, 2005). Interestingly, stereotypes premised on the degradation of African heritage females to protect the ego and esteem of slave owners have continued to shape modern caricatures. To justify rape and abuse of slave women and female children, they were accused of being more lustful, uninhibited, hot-blooded, and sexually loose than European American women (i.e., The Jezebel). Yet female slaves were forced to become pregnant early and rewarded for giving birth to numerous children, but emotional attachments were ignored when their children were beaten or sold to other plantations (i.e., Welfare Queen). In general, Black women were characterized as innately "strong," resilient, and impervious to pain or suffering to promote similar work load and performance expectations for males and females with the purpose being to enhance wealth regardless of gender even during pregnancy (i.e., Strong Black Woman). Those who primarily labored in the plantation house in close proximity to the master were depicted as devoted, nurturing, asexual, deferential, and selfless (i.e., Mammy). However such descriptions were not intended to accurately portray these women but to protect European Americans from the discomfort that awareness of their abuse produced and to justify the continued mistreatment of Black women (West, 1995). These stereotypes also differentiated female slaves from women of European descent, who were conversely constructed as weak, fragile, helpless, and virginal or chaste, which authorized the need for European male control and domination. Different historical periods have yielded other images of Black women. For instance, Sapphire was created during the forties and fifties based on a character on the *Amos 'n' Andy* show to depict women who were willing to express negative feelings and to fight for control of their bodies and personal space but cast as hostile, loud, angry, and controlling (Thomas, Witherspoon, & Speight, 2004). Beginning in the late seventies, youth and working-class popular culture contributed to diverse contemporary representations of African-American women shown in hip-hop/rap music videos. Stephens and Few (2007) examined African-American adolescent's subjective understandings of eight sexual images and found these conceptual frameworks influence their beliefs about physical appearance and interpersonal interactions (e.g., Gold Digger, Freak, Diva, Dyke, Baby Mama, Earth Mother, Sister Savior, and Gangsta Bitch). While critics view these images as sexually exploitative and misogynistic, some producers and performers portray themselves as independent and self-reliant (Emerson, 2002). This gender role legacy has contributed to modern cultural differences in meanings and demonstrations of womanliness and womanhood. Unfortunately, these stereotypical gender role images have led to the use of pejorative descriptors (e.g., domineering, tough, hard, matriarch, and bitch) to sustain the portrayal of Black women as the scapegoat for socioeconomic disparities between men of African and European descent (e.g., Staples, 1979).

The gendered role of the male slave, like his female counterpart, was largely determined by biology. Fathers of slave children were of little value beyond the necessary function of impregnation. They were not required, expected, nor typically allowed to maintain prolonged involvement as providers of emotional support to the mother, to serve as caretakers of children or protect mothers and children from danger or threat. A child was designated as "mother's baby, daddy's maybe" and race/ethnicity or social status of the father was insignificant because a bonded woman could only give birth to a bonded child. Male slaves were rendered ineffectual and powerless because of social and economic barriers that prevented fulfillment of male role requirements according to European patriarchal standards of masculinity and manhood. Consequently, physicality and the body (i.e., strength, stamina) became central to internalized meanings of manhood for the male slave and evaluations of Black manliness for the European American master.

These experiences have produced a European American cognitive schema of "Blackness" in which dark skin is associated with danger, threat, aggression, and violence with assumptions of sensuality and hyper-sexuality. African-American men are particularly viewed as uncontrolled, sex-starved savages who seek to ravage the purity of the sexually naïve European American female. Race and gender disconnections in this belief system attribute Black male-White female sexual interactions to Black male prowess but disregard sexual assaults committed against Black women by European American men. Assumptions specific to this schema produce expectancies of violence and brutality that arouse deep seated fear and anxiety reactions which in turn, elicit unbridled White rage responses. More importantly, because of the strength of the association between African-American men and negativity in the "Blackness" schema any behavior can be used interchangeably with the race/ethnic classification of African American to arouse malice and bitterness. For instance, the mere presence of a young African heritage male (especially if dressed in popular urban attire) can provoke the unconscious but ever-present insecurities and unbridled rage of European American police officers because dark skin has been connected to violence or sexual aggression. This response pattern is especially relevant to the numerous murders of Black males and females (e.g., Eric Garner, Michael Brown, Tamir Rice, Eric Harris, Sandra Bland) that gave rise to "Black Lives Matter," a movement which began with the jury acquittal of George Zimmerman for the death of Trayvon Martin in 2013 (Yancy, 2016). According to conservative Ben

Stein in remarks during an interview with Steve Malzberg in reference to Michael Brown, he stated, "He wasn't unarmed. He was armed with his incredibly strong, scary self" (Blue, 2014).

Early theorists linked European American's preparedness to express violence and hatred towards African Americans to an unconscious obsession with sex and feelings of sexual jealousy and competition toward Black men (e.g., Staples, 1971; Vontress, 1971). In response to African-American intellectual accomplishments and economic and political success and achievements (e.g., voting, political participation, business development, education attainment), European Americans reacted with violence and destruction which included the lynching of African-American males; although women were lynched as well. The potency of White male sexual jealousy became most obvious after intermarriage was legally prohibited between Black slave men and European women of indentured servitude. Lynching became the aggressive retort to break the will and motivation of Black men because of feelings of rage aroused by sexual competition. These murders were usually explained as revenge or punishment for the alleged sexual aggression displayed by African-American men toward White females. However, Ida B. Wells's published research showed that interracial sexual relations were most often consensual and typically initiated by European American women although viewed as socially unacceptable (Tucker, 1971). Therefore, lynching and the threat of lynching were used to indirectly control White female sexual attraction with punishment rather than allow them to openly acknowledge their interest in and attraction to men of African descent. A significant percentage of Black males accused of having relationships with White females were even lynched between 1890 and 1900 in West Virginia, a state originally thought to differ from southern states such as Mississippi, Louisiana, Georgia, and Texas (Konhaus, 2007; Wiegman, 1993). An antecedent to the Civil Rights Movement in 1955 was the murder of Emmet Till, a 14-year-old summer visitor to Mississippi from Chicago who disregarded the "White woman" warning of his mother and was alleged to have jokingly referred to a married European American woman as "baby" or whistled at her as he departed a store in response to a dare from friends. After he was forced to walk down a road and remove his clothing, he received a severe beating and a bullet to the head before being lynched. Timothy Tyson (2017), author of *The Blood of Emmet Till*, interviewed the now 72-year-old wife (i.e., Carolyn Bryant) of one of the men responsible for his murder who admitted that her testimony on the stand that he grabbed and verbally threatened her were both falsifications.

Through the years the media and research have promoted oppositional images based on stereotypical assumptions about African Americans; particularly African-American males. Cooper (2006) categorizes contemporary representations of African-American men according to "good Black man" and "bad Black man" anchors. The "good Black man" is "passive, nonassertive, and nonaggressive," remains separate from other Black people, and is assimilated into European mainstream culture. The "bad Black man" is stereotyped as "animalistic, crime-prone and sexually unrestrained," seen as marginal and unable to assimilate, and likely to receive more harsh consequences because of being seen as a threat (Ross, 1998). These images have been used to influence judicial and legal matters.

In the summer of 1989 Charles "Chuck" Stewart, a wealthy European American, made a false report that a Black man shot him and killed his wife and unborn son during a Massachusetts robbery. This news led Boston police to use "stop and frisk" to search more than a hundred men per day within the first five days of the case. They later discovered from his brother that Stewart killed his own wife and child. This case was fueled by fears of Blackness and stereotypes of Black men as "aggressive" and "predator" as every Black man became a suspect with many stopped by police and illegally searched, thereby dividing Boston along race/ethnic lines (Butterfield & Hays, 1990).

These cultural images have been valuable to those who have needed to inspire European American citizens for personal and political purposes. For example, George H. W. Bush successfully used photographs of and commercials about William R. "Willie" Horton, an African-American man, to reduce the lead of Michael Dukakis, the Democratic presidential candidate from Massachusetts in 1988. The country was bombarded with Horton's mugshot. Horton, who was then serving a life sentence for murder and rape of a White female, was on release as part of a weekend furlough program ("George Bush and Willie Horton," 1988). This image elicited fears that the "silent White majority" held about the "menacing" Black male criminal with an insatiable sexual desire to rape White women and girls and motivated voters to change the direction of the campaign from Dukakis who was viewed as "soft" on crime in favor of Bush. A similar ad that played upon White America's fear of Black male sexual prowess and interest in White women was used in 2006 to impede the course of the State Senate election in Tennessee of African-American Democratic nominee, Harold Ford, Jr., against European American Bob Corker as GOP candidate (Toner, 2006; "Harold Ford not for Tennessee," 2006). In this commercial sponsored by the Republican National Committee, several citizens speak about reasons *he* was "not right" but the final scene interjects Black male and female sexual involvement to arouse anxiety when a blond female is shown who whispers in a sensual tone "Harold, call me."

More recently, in 2015 Dylann Roof, a White male sat among members at a historically Black church during bible study in June 2015 for an hour before he killed nine African-American attendees for which he was found guilty in December 2016 (33 counts of federal hate crimes) (Blinder & Sack, 2016). He had allowed a Black female to live who testified that before taking the first shot, he said "they [African Americans] are taking over and taking all our women."

Racism and prejudice predicated principally on unconscious sexual rivalry of European heritage males seemingly became even more intense with the election of a president who was the male offspring of marriage between an African father and European-American mother. To fully comprehend the impact of the election of a self-identified African-American man and his family to the presidency of the United States in 2008 and 2012, it is necessary to consider the intersection of race and gender role ideologies.

Presidents and Hegemonic Masculinity

Research shows that the preferred characteristics of leaders are congruent with those culturally ascribed to males as masculinity but mismatched with the positive (e.g., compassionate, kind) and negative attributes (e.g., passive, emotional) attributed to females as femininity (Koenig, Eagly, Mitchell, & Ristikari, 2011). However only a few empirical studies are published that examine the masculinity and femininity of politicians in the realm of politics, political discourse and presentation of politicians (e.g., Winter, 2010). The duties and responsibilities associated with the European American cultural standard of father and the process of fathering have historically been attached to the presidency. The president's role as the masculine ideal of protector and leader rests upon the ideology of patriarchy. Despite American cultural values that espouse independence, self-reliance, individualism, and a bootstrap approach to achievement and success, an American president is sought to serve as a protector, leader, and hero who demonstrates concern for the well-being of citizens; an approximation of an ideal father figure to hold the position as Commander in Chief (Frame, 2012; Jeffords, 1994; Orman, 1987). Concerns about the adequacy of a candidate's attributes to serve as father to the nation are implied in assessments of the meaning and appropriateness of masculinity specific to the character and nature of presidential candidates. To this extent, gender stereotypes of the political parties have important weight in predicting how the public will evaluate a candidate or elected president.

Gendered role descriptors stereotypical of femininity are linked at the conscious and preconscious level of thought for Democratic supporters and attributes of traditional masculinity have become associated with values of Republican viewers. Winter (2010) used national election data and found evidence of such connections at the explicit level made for each party and at the implicit level for each connection. For example, attempts were made by Republicans to associate John Kerry with descriptors of femininity (Duerst-Lahti, 2008) and Al Gore was seen as falling short of meeting masculine standards because of an alleged low level of dominance (Duerst-Lahti, 2008). The presidency of George W. Bush required attitudes and behaviors consistent with an exaggerated European American masculinity to satisfy the American people because of the overarching threat of war and mayhem. The destructive and violent actions of terrorism and war inadvertently demanded that political leaders demonstrate gender role qualities that showed allegiance to a traditional masculine ideology. Bush's masculinity steeped in traditionalism and essentialism adhered to during his administration has been represented as capable, competent and able to handle crises more in line with traditionalist masculinity. Throughout 1999, for example, pollsters rated Bush as "a strong and decisive leader" (Burrell, 2008). Ronald Reagan, a man of older years was also heralded as high in masculinity, which may have been more party bound (i.e., Republican) than related to his personal qualities. An analysis of the 44th President as heir and progeny of John F. Kennedy proposes that "image-makers, have cannily refashioned this image to infuse Obama's own message of hope and change with an historical antecedent" (Frame, 2012, p. 17). According to Frame's (2012) comparison on personality, presentational style, and family status, both men represent the masculine good father as expected of the President of the United States. However, unlike John F. Kennedy, throughout his inauguration and elections, the personal qualities and family commitment of the 44th President were exemplary (Michaux, 2013).

Masculinity and the 44th President

Many perceived the 44th President as a man of mystery; partly because of his complicated persona and complex personality presented as self-controlled but authentic, emotionally expressive, intelligent, charming, charismatic, and intelligent but humorous; making it difficult to pigeon hole him into a specified set of masculine criteria. Prior to the 2008 election, many in the media characterized his values and worldviews and even mannerisms as feminine because they emphasized spirituality, inclusion, compassion and empathy and he presented as emotionally expressive, self-assured, relaxed, calm, and accommodating. Interpretations of his values and presentational style as culturally feminine led to the presumption of weak leadership which was strengthened by the stereotypical feminine characteristics typically associated with the Democratic party (e.g., soft on crime, afraid of war).

Criticisms of the 44th President originated from distorted perceptions of the relationship between gender role attributes and racial identification. He was presented as deficient in masculinity, weak, unwilling to "get tough" or demonstrate hardness and was in fact often characterized as too willing to allow foreign "others" to invade America because he was a marginal man and not really "one of the boys." According to Cooper (2009), during the 2008 Presidential campaign, a newspaper columnist posited, "If Bill Clinton was once considered America's first Black president, Obama may one day be viewed as our first woman president." He was even labeled as gay or homosexual to further emasculate and de-masculine him in a way consistent with the traditional masculine approach used to demean males who deviate from hegemonic masculine sanctioned behavioral norms. To persuade viewers that he did not meet the "good father" expectancy of an American and world leader it was necessary to convince the public that he was low in the masculine qualities (e.g., dominance, toughness) required for effective leadership as President (Eror, 2012). Republican reliance upon evaluations of hegemonic masculinity and party affiliation predicted similar expected outcomes for his stand on policy and international diplomacy. This assessment of the 44th President as leader and decision maker ignored the intersection of an African heritage race/ethnicity with party affiliation and gender role orientation and mistakenly typecast him as inadequate and ill-equipped to lead the country. Yet because of the gendered construction of racism, any display of toughness or dominance would have given way to accusations of the "angry Black man stereotype" (Wingfield, 2007). European-American conservatives also critiqued him negatively because of his unwillingness to accept their requirement of color-blindness and to distance himself from people of color. However, "Republicans mistake prudence for weakness. Obama's statecraft may lack the hard edges and black-and-white absolutes of his predecessor's, but the abandonment of ideological excess in favor of principled pragmatism is, perhaps, the greatest asset of Obama's diplomacy" (Kupchan & Jentleson, p. 15, 2012).

Many of the unconscious beliefs that have followed African-American men since slavery were ignited during both campaigns and presidencies For instance, stereotypes such as violent, aggressive, intellectually dull, inarticulate, marginal to society, and even unclean were introduced early with comments offered by Joe Biden in 2007 to show his strong *support* of the presidential candidate:

"I mean, you got the first mainstream African-American who is articulate and bright and clean and a nice-looking guy. I mean, that's a storybook, man." (Montopolic, 2007)

These were not the words of an overt bigot or self-identified racist, yet he seemed oblivious to the numerous African heritage men and women who had clearly met these "storybook" criteria. Here, Biden clarified how the presidential candidate adhered to the "good Black man" image which differentiated him from other African heritage men to make him acceptable to skeptical European heritage voters. However his comments also made it clear that even the most highly educated European-Americans have little awareness and knowledge of men of African-American descent other than the stereotypical portrayals reflected in the media.

The 44th President introduced a meaning of manhood to the nation that did not fulfill the traditional European-American hegemonic definition of masculinity. During both terms he performed gendered role behaviors which made obvious his adherence to masculine meanings of both African-American and European-American cultural norms. During both terms, his adherence to a gendered role that integrated elements traditionally stereotyped as feminine and masculine was made obvious. This diunital (i.e., union of opposites) gender role pattern was similar to the President's biracial heritage as contrasted with the fixed and immutable polarized pattern of European-American gender role norms. He demonstrated the capacity to integrate communication, interactional and behavioral styles that embodied aspects of traditional European masculine standards promoted by historians such as Frazier (1957) and Moynihan (1965), and Black militants/nationalists (e.g., Malcolm X) of the mid-sixties (Dyson, 1996). However his performance of manliness and masculinity transcended this masculine ideology, which relied upon bipolar masculine norms. His gender role enactment of masculinity also differed from and surpassed attributes associated with Black male alternative masculine standards (Harris & Majors, 1993; Harris, 1995) and thus, extended far beyond stereotypical images that defined Black manhood as sexual predator, aggressor, or absent father without denying his African heritage consistent with a "transformational" masculine ideology.

The 44th President disregarded traditional masculine norms and Black male alternative masculine behaviors related to race and gender role ideology in the selection of a wife and mother for his children. He chose a highly educated woman of African-American descent who approximated him in physical height and wielded higher earning power during their dating years. She was selected to serve as a partner and intellectual equal with the ability and skill to critique the President's speeches after his election, navigate social dynamics of the White House and independently establish relationships with the American public. Media members chose both race and gender narratives to present the 44th President and First Lady as threats to European Americans. European American adherence to a polarized relationship between masculine and feminine that constructs differences as fixed and immutable, requires that any behaviors and attributes of females (i.e., First Lady) embody reverse meanings to complement or confirm the dominance and control of the male (i.e., 44th President). For instance, the construction of masculine and feminine as bipolar opposites in European-American culture posited that if Michelle Obama was assertive, confident, and empowered, then the 44th President must be passive, ineffectual, and powerless or substandard.

Femininity and the First Lady

A European-American conception of femininity socially constructed as demur, delicate, deferential, or weak, childlike and indecisive, and the relative opposite of a hegemonic masculinity based in protection and strength or toughness partly explains the hostile reaction to First Lady Michelle Obama during the 2008 Democratic campaign (Thornton, 2010). Consequently, the First Lady received several scathing personal attacks couched in ridicule and disparagement. When she declared, "For the first time in my adult lifetime, I am really proud of my country, and not just because Barack has done well, but because I think people are hoping for change" (Sullivan, 2012, p. 54), segments of the public quickly and forcibly rose to humiliate her with micro-aggressions (e.g., Barack's "bitter half, "Mrs. Grievance"). Antipathy for the self-reliance, assertiveness, and independence descriptors of Black women were evident in the persistent use of aspersions cast to silence Michelle Obama.

These criticisms were used to alleviate discomfort caused by her authenticity and directness; qualities unacceptable to European American constructions of womanhood and femininity. Michelle Obama was discussed in-depth because of her novelty as the first African-American woman to serve as First Lady of the United States. This attribute made her different from previous women in this position and brought with it stereotypical expectations associated with the intersection of race/ethnicity and gender.

First, with the exception of Hillary Clinton, First Lady Michelle Obama was the most highly educated of all First Ladies and earned a doctorate in law from Harvard University. She also differed from previous First Ladies in other ways. Unlike the majority of her predecessors, she entered the White House as mother to two young daughters with the responsibilities of being a wife. According to Gilkes (2010) both Michelle Obama and Jacqueline Kennedy (Onassis) were marginal and had to prove their value as First Ladies to the public. The obsessive gaze used to dissect and assess their appropriateness for the position overwhelmingly centered on physical appeal, style, and attire. However, monocultural beauty criteria were used to gauge the appearance of Michelle Obama. Body norms and beauty ideals affiliated with the femininity of females of European descent were inappropriately applied to critique her adequacy as first lady. Early on during their first campaign for office the public concentrated on her body with greater positive and negative attention than her education or parenting. They particularly developed an obsessive fascination with the shape of her body and muscularity of her arms. Her statuesque presentation, brown skin, and physically toned and curvaceous physique differentiated her from the typical White females displayed in the media, which, in turn, ironically introduced questions about her qualifications and suitability for the role of the First Lady. Women expressed envy and interest in how to achieve a similar degree of fitness in an outpour of discussion about the muscularity of her arms, but these physical assets were interpreted as liabilities and used to infer an absence of femininity when it benefited critics. Contempt for egalitarian African-American gender role interactions that failed to celebrate a less educated, passive, smiling female alongside a dominating, controlling, macho, stoic male was epitomized in the development of a highly disrespectful video that raised the question, "Michele Obama is transgender man?" (Jones, 2016). In this video, it was alleged that the First Lady's original name was Michael and that she did not give birth to her two daughters. She was assumed to have been born a biological male and became a transgendered man who had future plans for sexual reassignment surgery. At the same time that some declined to accept the biological femaleness of the First Lady, others such as Bob Grisham of Alabama, Rush Limbaugh, and Congressman James Sensenbrenner (R-Wisconsin) attended to her curvaceous build with inappropriate comments (e.g., "Fat-butt Michelle Obama," Michelle "My-Butt" Obama, "large posterior" ("Why White men are obsessed with the First Lady's Butt," 2013). Still others in the social media community referred to her as "gorilla in heels" and "ape" and used the phrase "*Moo*-chelle" to equate her body with animals (Allen, 2016). Such racist discourse has been used historically as Black women's bodies are evaluated through the culturally biased gaze of European Americans who disparage them in order to deny and avoid unwanted feelings of envy and attraction, and "reflect a continued hard-core anti-Blackness" (Gilkes, 2010, p. 74).

An affectionate and playful fist bump or pound shared with her husband was only another instance of misrepresentation or distortion of a nonverbal communication gesture that heightened the already abnormal anxiety of European Americans who saw the couple as "foreign" or "different." This exchange was wrongfully equated with a "terrorist communication" by E. D. Hill, a Fox News anchor (Rutenberg, 2008). The race and gender stereotype of the First Lady as the angry one, an afro-wearing militant armed with an assault weapon encouraged even greater uneasiness and distress among mainstream European Americans. Questions about how she would function in the White House were only put to rest later in the first term after she self-identified as "mom-in-chief" and engaged in "community other mothering" (King, 2010), which encompassed all of the traditional female gender stereotypes of caretaker, nurturer, and wife and which, in turn, partly offset her qualities as assertive, competent, intelligent, and career oriented. The need to view her as submissive and nonthreatening rather than powerful and personally empowered was thoroughly accomplished as she engaged in fewer discussions about the needs of Americans, reported having little interest in the president's decisions, and concentrated primarily on their children and children of the nation. These decisions and behaviors indirectly silenced the noise and reduced fears about the emasculation of the 44th President in relation to the competence of the First Lady but aroused suspicion given her emphasis on mothering full time. The decision to focus on her daughters and to place their well-being and adjustment ahead of other personal and social alternatives challenged the historical normative of the Black Super Woman. Yet, First Lady Obama asserted power and status in her embrace of extended and fictive kin systems that supported collectivism in the socialization of her biological children and those of mothers throughout the nation rather than in the portrayal of the individualistic, nuclear family form as the primary unit of child socialization. Andre Leon Talley *Vogue*'s editor at large, described Mrs. Obama as "the most transformative first lady in history (Talley, 2009). She became a beauty and fashion icon who gave opportunities and exposure to many new designers who selected her to showcase their clothing. Likewise, she promoted the importance of physical fitness and healthy eating for children and adults in the face of criticism directed at her body and appearance. Consistent with a Black cultural orientation of inclusiveness and diversity, she also recreated the White House as open to all Americans with an emphasis on community (e.g., Turnaround Arts) (Slevin, 2016).

The 44th President, Masculinity and Fathering

Central to the 44th President's enactment of masculinity were the roles of husband and father performed in relation to the First Lady and his daughters, respectfully. Despite responsibilities and a busy schedule of appointments, he was fully present and emotionally and psychologically accessible and available to his wife and children, America, and the world. The 44th President's performance of manhood challenged the persistent stereotypical depictions of Black fathers as physically and emotionally unavailable and financially absent (e.g., Moynihan, 1965).

His masculine identification evolved from introspection undertaken to navigate experiences in the passage to manhood clearly described in *Dreams from My Father* (Obama, 2007). His effort to critique and examine his sense of self in relation to a physically absent father to determine where he should stand in American society as a biracial man was crucial to the African-American community. Reflections on questions of personal identity and manliness are especially pivotal for single mothers of young sons who lack daily access to fathers and fathers who have little or no relationship with their children. Interestingly, the president's election demonstrated that even a physically absent biological father can serve to motivate a child's future success. However, the president did not embrace or internalize the obvious hegemonic masculine identity but produced a new or transformed masculinity that included the intersection of multiple voices rather than the exclusion of those traditionally seen as threatening. As a father, he incorporated and valued the importance of communication, collaboration, and role shifting rather than a predominant dependence on masculine norms. His interpersonal comfort and self-confidence provided the foundation for open interactions with his daughters and wife and emotional responsiveness through friendliness, kindness, humor, and public affection. During his adolescence and young adulthood, prior to marriage and family, he learned to interact with women without the gauge of sexism and inequality typically equated with masculinity. This particular construction of manhood manifested in displays of sensitivity, respect, empathy, and demonstrations of concern that disputed traditional masculine beliefs and behaviors steeped in dominance and control.

Despite the need of the president to fulfill the dreams of his father, the journey undertaken in his book was paved with guidance from intelligent and confident women. The path itself was framed and designed by his biological mother (Stanley Ann Dunham) who offered him a "dream" or framework for living that included character, integrity, and leadership against the backdrop of the unconditional love and support of grandparents, including a grandmother who served as the primary family breadwinner (i.e., vice-president of a bank). His mother dismissed the facts of her relationship with his biological father, Barack Sr., and intentionally omitted his personal attributes and any marital experiences that might distress her son or cause him to turn inward in shame or develop feelings of low esteem. She offered instead a *modified* image seemingly based on perceptions of her ex-husband's most esteemed qualities (e.g., intelligence, motivation) to drive her son's aspirations. Her bond with the future 44th President allowed her to implant core values of an early masculine identity comprised of achievement, courage, and fairness. Stanley Ann Dunham also shared strengths of African-American culture through works of literature, middle-class leaders, and music that initiated development of her son's African-American racial identity. During their time in Indonesia with her second husband (i.e., Lolo Soetoro) she integrated African-American history with *modified stories* or myths about his father to counteract teachings of his stepfather that men must conceal their emotions as an aspect of masculinity (Anthony, 2013). Through her gifts of values, beliefs, and cultural icons, his mother encouraged him to develop cognitive schemata for Blackness and masculinity through which all future experiences and interactions would be interpreted, compared, and critiqued.

Consistent with a transformational masculine identity, the 44th President disagreed with meanings of hegemonic masculinity proposed by Black nationalists and viewed them as dangerous to the African-American family, community, and male peer relationships. He rejected, in particular, the way in which some men of African descent choose to assert racially gendered power and privilege in their interactions with women (Collins, 2005; Hoston, 2014). The 44th President's enactment of Blackness and masculinity were discordant with the traditional stereotypical images of Blackness because of the intersection of social status, education, appearance, and personality with racial descent. For a minority of European Americans, the intersection of these qualities with his biracial heritage reduced the racial and gender stigma of "Black male" and demonstrated acknowledgment, if not acceptance, of biracial children and interracial families. However, the ease with which the president performed made it possible to forget the negative stereotypes attributed to "Black" and biracial, and frightened those high in racism and prejudice which fueled "White rage" that had been dormant for years (Anderson, 2016). Rage that emerged from the threat of loss of White privilege produced greater disrespect for this Commander in Chief than any other presidents sworn into this position and accompanied an unprecedented number of abusive and insulting comments levied at the 44th President, the First Lady, and their children.

The marginalization of "others" (e.g., minority men, gay men, women) and the need to control women associated with the traditional hegemonic European American masculinity motivated the 44th President to reject many aspects of the traditional gender role ideology (Ling, 2005). In addition, he recognized that Black alternative masculinities are inadequate for the development and proper functioning of African-American families. African-American gender role ideologies adapted in the post-Civil Rights era that constructed men as weak and incompetent and females as strong and competent were also seen as inappropriate for parenting and family development (Collins, 2005).

However, the athletic image enacted by the 44th President during both terms confirmed the connection between sports and masculinity portrayed in the media and supported by research. Masculinity studies suggest that men use sports and athletic participation and interests to identify primarily with other males (Moore & Dewberry, 2012). Specifically, their success or failure establishes ranking in the socially constructed masculine hierarchy in which athleticism involves physical competence and competition (Carroll, 2003). The 44th President's participation in basketball and golf, but particularly his passion for the former, demonstrated his ability to lead and dominate on the court, which epitomized the sport-masculine ideal connection and generalized it to the presidential arena. During the first term, his interest in basketball served as a conduit for the development of relationships with African-American males (e.g., major basketball players, male youth) (Fletcher, 2016) and the American public because of the sport's centrality to popular culture. By the second term he engaged in less basketball playing but continued to remain physically active with a monthly increase in playing golf (Fletcher, 2016).

Fathering and Masculinity

The 44th President's lifestyle and behavior as husband and father provided an alternative to the historical stereotypical depictions of Black manhood. There is perhaps little of greater relevance to the African-American community that needs intervention than family functioning and effective parenting. For instance, in Chicago where large numbers of Black males face high unemployment, gang violence, and high dropout and low progression rates, more than 69% of fathers are considered "absent" from home (Hoston, 2014). Mothers depend on their sons and often relate to them as fathers/husbands rather than children. This makes it difficult for males to fulfill their roles as youth when they sacrifice their childhoods to support mothers and siblings (Hoston, 2014).

Several factors contribute to the general perception that African-American fathers are inaccessible and uncaring. The importance of the role of provider to traditional hegemonic masculinity is significant to this assumption. Fathering is most associated with instrumental functions of which financial support and responsibility are central criteria in European American culture. However the inability of young fathers to provide economic and financial support for their children makes it difficult for them to adhere to this aspect of traditional masculinity. Related to this role is the need for employment. However African-American males of all age groups experience a significantly higher rate of unemployment and underemployment, which reduces available income. The higher rate of children born to unmarried parents adds to their financial burden to care for their individual needs and meet the needs of children who often reside in a different location. The likelihood of unemployment and low earnings related to lower educational levels increases the risk of participation in activities that can result in contact with the judicial system, and possible conviction and incarceration. Together, these factors contribute to greater father inaccessibility during children's development. Given that these numbers have continued to increase through the years, stereotypical interpretations of the role of African-American fathers have persisted. This state of affairs is exacerbated by a limited number of African-American father images in the media.

Only a few fathers of African-American descent in the media have been shown through the years to have positive relationships with children and families. For instance, Julius Rock (*Everybody Hates Chris*), James Evans Sr. (*Good Times*), Judge Philip "Uncle Phil" Banks (*Fresh Prince of Bel-Air*), officer Carl Winslow (*Family Matters*), Joseph Rev. Run (*Run's House*), Dre Johnson (*Black-ish*), George Jefferson (*The Jeffersons*), and Fred G. Sanford (*Sanford & Son*) comprise most of the positive African-American father images shown on television (Sharp, 2014). However, the impact of these fathers has seemingly been minor relative to images that depict fathers of Black heritage as ineffective and uninvolved. The traditional and historical stereotypical narrative of African-American fathers as uncaring, irresponsible, and absent has continued into the twenty-first century.

Based on the 44th President's construction of masculinity, he made it clear in public forums and addresses that many of the issues that plague the African-American community relate to the scarcity of *two* parents' involvement in childrearing. He especially emphasized the role of fathering in the lives of African-American males. Given his realization that two-parent families in the form of legal marriage are hardly a panacea for life success and that marriage cannot erase racism and sexism, the 44th President never encouraged this particular lifestyle to resolve family problems. Yet the centrality of his father's absence created a desire to enact a meaning of masculinity in connection to family and community that also inspired sensitivity to the need for father involvement. The 44th President's strong stance on the importance of fathering for healthy families and child development indirectly encouraged men of African-American descent to disregard harsh portrayals of them shown in the media and assumed by the public and to engage in responsible fathering. His decision to open dialogue on this topic countered beliefs about uncaring African-American fathers and established routes through which greater father engagement and more effective fathering could occur. These beliefs about families and fathers were noted in his Father's Day speech given at the Apostolic Church of God in Chicago in 2008. In this speech he openly acknowledged the impact of father absence on Black families as he presented fathers as critical to the well-being and healthy functioning of the family system:

> But if we are honest with ourselves, we'll admit that too many fathers also are missing—missing from too many lives and too many homes. They have abandoned their responsibilities, acting like boys instead of men. And the foundations of our families are weaker because of it. You and I know how true this is in the African American community. (*New York Times*, Obama, 2008)

The 44th President used his experience as a child and adolescent who grew into manhood without his biological father to enhance his commitment as a father to his children. He also maintained the hope that his fathering behaviors might serve to model a lifestyle that young men could emulate. In 2008 in an interview with *Ladies Home Journal*, he stated:

> As somebody who didn't grow up with a father in the home, I like having men come up to me saying, "You know, I'm really glad you're a good father." I like that maybe some little boy somewhere who doesn't have a dad in his house sees Michelle and the girls and me out somewhere and is going to carry that image in his head with him somewhere down the road. (Block, 2016)

As a senator, Barack Obama supported a program called the Responsible Fatherhood and Healthy Families Act. Following his 2008 election, he created a task force and modified a government website related to fathering and fatherhood. He also created a public information service (i.e., Fatherhood Buzz). The 44th President initiated Federal programs with the objective to increase father involvement in families. On June 19, 2009, the Responsible Fatherhood and Healthy Families Act was presented as a policy to enhance father participation. This act provides grants to parents of lower social status for economic opportunities, establishes career/jobs that require educational training, addresses the debt of unpaid child support, reverses the federal funding cuts of child support programs, requires all the collected child support to be paid to the families, expands the Earned Income Tax Credit (EITC), and repeals the child-support fee charged to parents (Civic Impulse, 2017).

In 2009 the Fatherhood Educational Institute (FEI) announced the 44th President as the recipient of "Father of the Year Award," an award that honors the "finest examples of American fatherhood" to recognize his work to increase the presence of fathers in the family system and family involvement (Lee, 2010). On June 15, 2011, the White House also sponsored a Strong Fathers, Strong Families initiative to involve American companies and organizations with the objective to involve fathers by offering discounts to men who took their children to various events (e.g., sports, bowling, the zoo) (Strautmanis, 2011).

In 2012 he extended the meaning of father beyond biology and discussed the many roles and responsibilities of those who serve as father models:

> For many of us, our fathers show us by the example they set the kind of people they want us to become. Whether biological, foster, or adoptive, they teach us through the encouragement they give, the questions they answer, the limits they set, and the strength they show in the face of difficulty and hardship. (Obama, 2012)

Second, the 44th President's relationship with his children demonstrate that African-American fathers are indeed involved in quality parenting of their children. He displayed consistency in his thoughts and beliefs about fathering and fatherhood during both terms and in interviews and speeches, and he willingly shared personal experiences regarding his role as a father. In his interviews he made it clear that he was proud of his daughters and genuinely liked them. In 2012 he described them as "strong, smart and beautiful young women, just like your mom." He openly shared his feelings of loss and sadness at the thought of his oldest daughter (Malia) leaving to attend college and described her as "one of my best friends." In an interview on *The Tonight Show* starring Jimmy Fallon in 2016, he also described them as "smart, funny and kind."

At the 2013 graduation ceremony for Morehouse College, the 44th President asked male graduates to revolutionize constructions of manhood and masculinity and "[t]o transform the way we think about manhood and set higher standards for ourselves and others":

> I'm asking all of you to . . . keep setting an example of what it means to be a man. Be the best husband to your wife, or boyfriend to your partner, or father to your children that you can be. Because nothing is more important.

The 44th President referred to the work and sacrifice of his mother and grandparents and the extended family of the males in the audience and then continued to emphasize the difference between present fathers and involved fathers.

> But I still wish I had a father who was not only present, but involved. And so my, whole life, I've tried to be for Michelle and my girls what my father wasn't for my mother and me. I've tried to be a better husband, a better father, and a better man.

In contrast to the competition and dominance shown in sport, the need for male camaraderie and support were encouraged. The young men were admonished to help other males along who may not have had the same opportunities; a theme similar in spirit to the objectives of his My Brother's Keeper program initiative (Horsley, 2016):

> Be a good role model and set a good example for that young brother coming up. If you know someone who isn't on point, go back and bring that brother along. The brothers who have been left behind—who haven't had the same opportunities we have—they need to hear from us. We've got to be in the barbershops with them, at church with them, spending time and energy and presence helping pull them up, exposing them to new opportunities, and supporting their dreams. We have to teach them what it means to be a man.

Empirical research conducted to examine father involvement with African-American male youth also increased since the 44th President's emphasis on fathering. Lawrence, Watson, and Stepteau-Watson (2013) used self-report to examine intergenerational father involvement of 68 men and found that men report spending more time with their children than their fathers spent with them whether fathers resided in the same or different residences. Ransaw (2014) investigated how nine African-American men attempt to be "good" fathers and the behaviors they use to assist their children with school, and found they use communication, focus on being a role model, and continue the role of fathering during and after their children's college enrollment (e.g., life and educational advice).

Actions and values of the 44th President support a transformational masculinity comprised of attributes and qualities associated with multiple masculinities rather than a single hegemonic masculine orientation. Ronald Reagan was presented as a masculine and formidable presidential leader by numerous conservatives. However, Sullivan (2012) described the 44th President as the "Democrat's Reagan" and proposed that both presidents achieved two large initial successes in their first term although the former did so in a "far worse economic and fiscal climate (p. 36). Since 2010, the 44th Presidential administration witnessed several achievements: "near obliteration of al Qaeda, democratic revolutions in the Arab world that George Bush could only have dreamed of, the re-regulation of Wall Street after the 2008 crash, stimulus investments in infrastructure and clean energy, powerful new fuel—immersion standards along with a record level of independence from foreign oil—and most critically, health care reform." (Sullivan, 2012, p. 33). His "own party embraced full marriage equality and integrated gays into the military" (p. 36). In general, each of these efforts can be categorized as representative of both masculine and feminine. After a mass shooting at Sandy Hook Elementary school in Connecticut in December, 2012, the 44th President revealed a proposal to address the use of guns in violence in the United States and encouraged Congress to pass legislation related to gun control (e.g., ban assault weapons, increase background check standards). On January 5, 2016, he once more discussed a new strategy to decrease gun violence which consisted of 23 executive actions that would require congressional approval (Sola, 2016).

Despite rather consistent criticism during the President's second term on foreign policy, his ideas associated with "Liberal"-International Relations theory benefited America. In general his actions and decisions embodied a realistic perspective that led to leadership based on morality and wisdom and that did not cause major problems for America that some of the more "masculine" presidents produced (Goldsmith, 2014). In comparison with other presidents, he did not make any significant mistakes, he improved the image of our country throughout the world as a diplomat, made hard decisions when necessary, and was willing to "forego bold statements for balanced probabilities" (Goldsmith, 2014). For instance, in his 2015 State of the Union Address to Congress he stated:

> My first duty as Commander-in-Chief is to defend the United States of America. In doing so, the question is not whether America leads in the world, but how. When we make rash decisions, reacting to the headlines instead of using our heads; when the first response to a challenge is to send in our military—then we risk getting drawn into unnecessary conflicts, and neglect the broader strategy we need for a safer, more prosperous world. That's what our enemies want us to do. I believe in a smarter kind of American leadership. We lead best when we combine military power with strong diplomacy; when we leverage our power with coalition building; when we don't let our fears blind us to the opportunities that this new century presents. That's exactly what we're doing right now—and around the globe, it is making a difference. (Miller, 2015)

Finally, the 44th President's observable actions were aligned with his beliefs and teachings about the significance of masculinity and fathering during both terms. He displayed warmth and affection toward his wife and daughters and engaged in proper social etiquette free from objectification, subjugation, and sexism. He also seemed at ease with himself and observers in demonstrations of affection, both physically and verbally, toward his wife and daughters. He frequently applauded the beauty and intelligence of the First Lady, praised his daughters, and teased them but espoused clear expectations for academic performance free of gender bias. He was willing to display affect and openly express emotions in socially appropriate ways and situations and did not hold to the belief that emotional expression and communication that involves a range of emotion is unacceptable for an adult man. Yet these actions and attitudes did not interfere with his ability to make effective and intelligent decisions, engage in direct and assertive communication, or participate in sport and athletic interests or worship and spirituality. Together, these behaviors distinguish him from previous American presidents and point to the value of a transformational masculinity comprised of character, integrity, and value rather than aggression, domination, and control.

Conclusion

The 44th President and the First Lady shifted the meaning of America and the American Dream from individualism and materialism to an emphasis on the role of community, family, and collective responsibility in the advancement of American society. "Just as Obama created a narrative that balanced personal and societal values and in so doing made the American dream more accessible to liberals . . ." (Rowland & Jones, 2007, p. 44), his enactment of a transformational masculinity has made manhood and masculinity accessible to more men and, consequently, moved to level the performance of masculinity for women who aspire to become president.

Important characteristics that should be added to masculinity are "fathering," "family focused," or "family centered." The decision to serve as a strong father, to love and support daughters as much as sons, for fathers to carve out a relationship with their daughters, to serve as husbands with highly educated wives, and to engage in emotional expressiveness and empathy without fear of reproach are potentially valuable qualities of transformational masculinity. In the future researchers should examine the findings of qualitative and quantitative research conducted during these years to examine how (if at all) perceptions of the 44th President's embodiment of masculinity during both terms influenced the gendered behaviors and attitudes of men of African descent. Research conducted to assess the impact of his years in office on how mothers of African descent socialize their sons, particularly related to career and education, are important given that this was the first time in history a Black male model was available to all male youth. Likewise, given the media's depiction of the relationship between the First Lady and the President and their daughters in the past years, how men and women of African descent conceptualized and constructed the meaning of relationship, marriage, and family would shed light on the 44th President's influence beyond the realm of politics (i.e., the Obama effect) (Marx, Ko & Friedman, 2009).

References

Allen, N. (2016, November 15). West Virginia official who called Michelle Obama an 'ape in heels' fired following outcry. *The Telegraph*. Retrieved from http://www.telegraph.co.uk/news/2016/11/15/michelle-obama-ape-in-heels-facebook-post-causes-outrage/

Anderson, C. (2016). *White rage: The unspoken truth of our racial divide*. Bloomsbury: New York.

Anthony, R. C. H. (2013). Searching for the new Black Man: Black masculinity and women's Bodies. Jackson, MI: University Press of Mississippi.

Binion, V. J. (1990). Psychological androgyny: A Black female perspective. *Sex Roles, 22*(7), 487–507.

Blinder, A., & Sack, K. (2016, December 15). Dylann Roof found guilty in Charleston church massacre. Retrieved from https://www.nytimes.com/2016/12/15/us/dylann-roof-trial.html?_r=0

Block, T. (2016, June 19). President Obama melts our hearts with quotes on fatherhood. Retrieved from https://www.popsugar.com/celebrity/photo-gallery/23530848/image/23530881/2008-Obama-talked-Ladies-Home-Journal-about-growing-up

Blue, M. (2014, August 27). Ben Stein: Michael Brown 'Wasn't Unarmed. He Was Armed With His Incredibly Strong, Scary Self.' Retrieved from http://www.rightwingwatch.org/post/ben-stein-michael-brown-wasnt-unarmed-he-was-armed-with-his-incredibly-strong-scary-self/

Brownstein, R. (2015, June 18). Obama, stuck in neutral. *The Atlantic*. Retrieved from https://www.theatlantic.com/politics/archive/2015/06/obamas-slow-recovery/396161/

Buckley, T. R., & Carter, R. T. (2005). Black adolescent girls: Do gender role and racial identity: Impact their self-esteem? *Sex Roles, 53*(9–10), 647–661.

Burrell, B. (2008). Likeable? Effective commander in chief? Polling on candidate traits in the "year of the presidential woman." *PS: Political Science & Politics, 41*(4), 747–752.

Butterfield, F., & Hays, C. L. (1990, January 15). A Boston tragedy: The Stuart Case—A special case; Motive remains a mystery in deaths that haunt a city (pg. A13). Retrieved from http://www.nytimes.com/1990/01/15/us/boston-tragedy-stuart-case-special-case-motive-remains-mystery-deaths-that-haunt.html?pagewanted=all

Carroll, B. (Ed.). (2003). *American masculinities: A historical encyclopedia*. Thousand Oaks, CA: SAGE.

Civic Impulse (2017). S. 1309—111th Congress: Responsible Fatherhood and Healthy Families Act of 2009. Retrieved from https://www.govtrack.us/congress/bills/111/s1309

Collins, P. H. (2005). *Black sexual politics: African Americans, gender, and the new racism*. New York: Routledge.

Cooper, F. R. (2006). Against bipolar Black masculinity: Intersectionality assimilation, identity performance, and hierarchy. *University of California at Davis Law Review, 38*, 853–906.

Cooper, F. R., "Our First Unisex President?: Black masculinity and Obama's feminine side" (2009). Suffolk University Law School Faculty Publications. Paper 52. http://lsr.nellco.org/suffolk_fp/52

Dorrien, G. (2012). *The Obama question: A progressive perspective*. Lanham: MD: Roman & Littlefield Publishers, Inc.

Duerst-Lahti, G. (2008). Seeing what has always been: Opening study of the presidency. *Political Science and Politics, 41*(4), 733–737.

Dyson, M. E. (1996). *Making Malcolm: The myth and meaning of Malcolm X*. New York: Oxford University Press on Demand.

Emerson, R. A. (2002). "Where my girls at?" Negotiating black womanhood in music videos. *Gender & Society, 16*(1), 115–135.

Eror. A. (2012, October 11). This man has proof that Obama is gay. Retrieved from https://www.vice.com/en_dk/article/this-man-has-proof-that-obama-is-gay

Fletcher, M. A. (2016, August 3). Obama, the aging athlete: *The president retreats from the physical intensity of basketball to the relative serenity of golf*. Retrieved from https://theundefeated.com/features/obama-the-aging-athlete/

Frame, G. (2012). Seeing Obama, projecting Kennedy: The presence of JFK in images of Barack Obama. *Comparative American Studies, 10* (2–3), 163–176.

Frazier, F. (1957). *Black Bourgeoisie*. New York: Free Press.

George Bush and Willie Horton. (1988, November 4). *The New York Times Opinion*. Retrieved from http://www.nytimes.com/1988/11/04/opinion/george-bush-and-willie-horton.html

Gilkes, C. T. (2010). Outsider within the higher circles: Two first ladies as cultural icons in a racialized politics of difference. In D. Cunnigen & M. M. Bruce (Eds.), *Race in the age of Obama* (pp. 55–75). United Kingdom: Emerald Publishers.

Goldsmith, B. E. (2014, October 6). A liberal defense of Barack Obama's foreign policy. Retrieved from http://www.e-ir.info/2014/10/06/a-liberal-defense-of-barack-obamas-foreign-policy/

Harold Ford Jr. (2006, October 22). Not for Tennessee. [Video File] Retrieved from https://www.youtube.com/watch?v=kkiz1_d1GsA

Harris, S. M. (1995). Psychosocial development and Black male masculinity: Implications for counseling economically disadvantaged African American male adolescents. *Journal of Counseling & Development, 73*, 279–287.

Harris, S. M., & Majors, R. (1993). Cultural value differences: Implications for the experiences of African-American men. *The Journal of Men's Studies, 1*(3), 227–238.

Hartmann, D. (2008). The social significance of Barack Obama. *Contexts, 7*(4), 16–21.

Horsley, S. (2016). Obama's Post-White House Plans Include My Brother's Keeper Effort Retrieved from http://www.npr.org/2016/12/26/507021405/obamas-post-white-house-plans-include-my-brothers-keeper-effort

Hoston, W. T. (2014). *Black masculinity in the Obama era: Outliers of society*. New York: Palgrave Macmillan.

Jeffords, S. (1994). *Hard bodies: Hollywood masculinity in the Reagan era*. New Brunswick, NJ: Rutgers University Press.

Jones, A. (2016, May 16). Alex Jones: Is Michelle Obama transgender? It would explain a lot. Retrieved from https://www.infowars.com/is-michelle-obama-transgender-2/

King, D. K. (2010). Mom-in-chief: Community othermothering and Michelle Obama, the first lady of the people's house. In D. Cunnigen & M. M. Bruce (Eds.), *Race in the Age of Obama* (pp. 77–123). Emerald Group Publishing Limited.

Koenig, A. M., Eagly, A. H., Mitchell, A. A., & Ristikari, T. (2011). Are leader stereotypes masculine? A meta-analysis of three research paradigms. *Psychological Bulletin, 137*(4), 616–642.

Konhaus, T. (2007). "I Thought Things Would Be Different There": Lynching and the Black Community in Southern West Virginia, 1880–1933. *West Virginia History: A Journal of Regional Studies, 1*(2), 25–43.

Kupchan, C., & Jentleson, B. (October & November, 2012). Obama's strong suit. *World Today, 68*(8/9), 15–16.

Lawrence, K. S., Watson, J., & Stepteau-Watson, D. (2013). President Obama and the fatherhood initiative. *Race, Gender & Class, 20*(3/4), 98–113.

Lee, J. (June 21, 2010). President Obama promotes responsible fatherhood: "No Excuses." Retrieved from https://obamawhitehouse.archives.gov/blog/2010/06/21/president-obama-promotes-responsible-fatherhood-no-excuses

Ling, P. J. (2005). Be a man, my son. *Reviews in American history, 33*(4), 601–606.

Marx, D. M., Ko, S. J., & Friedman, R. A. (2009). The "Obama effect": How a salient role model reduces race-based performance differences. *Journal of Experimental Social Psychology, 45*(4), 953–956.

Michaux, M. B. (2013). The first family: Transforming the American ideal. In J. S. Vaughn & L. J. Goren (Eds.), *Women and the White House: Gender, popular culture and presidential politics* (pp. 249–268). Lexington, KY: The University Press of Kentucky.

Miller, Z. J. (2015, January 21). Here's the Full Text of President Obama's 2015 State of the Union. *Time.* http://time.com/3675705/full-text-state-union-2015/

Montopolic, B. (2007, January 31). His Own Worst Enemy. *CBS News.* Retrieved from http://www.cbsnews.com/news/his-own-worst-enemy-2419103/

Moore, A. J., & Dewberry, D. (2013). The masculine image of presidents as sporting figures: A public relations perspective. *2*(3), https://doi.org/10.1177/2158244012457078

Morgan, D. (2007, February 10). Transcript of Barack Obama's speech. Retrieved from https://www.cbsnews.com/news/transcript-of-barack-obamas-speech/

Moynihan, D. P. (1965). *The Negro family: The case for national action.* Washington, DC: U. S. Department of Labor.

Obama, B. (2007). *Dreams from my father: A story of race and inheritance.* Edinburgh, Scotland: Canongate Books.

Obama, B. (2007). *The audacity of hope: Thoughts on reclaiming the American dream.* New York: Crown/Three Rivers Press.

Obama's father's day remarks. Retrieved from http://www.nytimes.com/2008/06/15/us/politics/15text-obama.html

Obama, B. (2012). Presidential Proclamation—Father's Day 2012. Retrieved from https://obamawhitehouse.archives.gov/the-press-office/2012/06/15/presidential-proclamation-father-s-day-2012

Obama, B. (2013, May 19). Prepared text for President Obama's speech at Morehouse. Retrieved from http://www.ajc.com/news/local/prepared-text-for-president-obama-speech-morehouse/82cVEdUTCaJA6SixsyKWIN/

Orman, J. (1987). *Comparing presidential behaviour: Carter, Reagan, and the macho presidential style*. New York: Greenwood University Press.

Ransaw, T. (2014). The good father: African American fathers who positively influence the educational outcomes of their children. *Spectrum: A Journal on Black Men 2*(2), 1–25.

Ross, M. B. (1998). In search of men's masculinities. *Feminist Studies, 24*(3), 599–626.

Rowland, R. C., & Jones, J. M. (2007). Recasting the American dream and American politics: Barack Obama's keynote address to the 2004 Democratic National Convention. *Quarterly Journal of Speech, 93*(4), 425–448.

Rutenberg, J. (2008, June 11). Deconstructing the bump. Retrieved from https://thecaucus.blogs.nytimes.com/2008/06/11/deconstructing-the-bump/?_r=0

Sharp, D. (2014, June 14). Black TV dads we wish would adopt us. *The Root*. Retrieved from http://www.theroot.com/black-tv-dads-we-wish-would-adopt-us-1790876057

Slevin, P. (2016, December 13). How Michelle Obama became a singular American voice. *The Washington Post*. Retrieved from https://www.washingtonpost.com/graphics/national/obama-legacy/michelle-obama-biography.html

Sola, K. (2016, January 6). Here Are Obama's New Executive Actions On Gun Control. *Forbes*. Retrieved from https://www.forbes.com/sites/katiesola/2016/01/06/obama-gun-control/#5d268c9d3f36

Staples, R. (1971). The myth of the impotent Black male. *The Black Scholar, 2*(10), 2–9.

Staples, R. (1979). The myth of Black macho: A response to angry Black feminists. *The Black Scholar, 10*(6–7), 24–33.

Strautmanis, M. (2011, June 15). Strong Fathers, Strong Families. Retrieved from https://obamawhitehouse.archives.gov/blog/2011/06/15/strong-fathers-strong-families

Stephens, D. P., & Few, A. L. (2007). The effects of images of African American women in hip hop on early adolescents' attitudes toward physical attractiveness and interpersonal relationships. *Sex Roles, 56*(3–4), 251–264.

Sullivan, A. (October, 2012). Welcome back to the White House Mr. President. *Newsweek*, 30–36.

Talley, A. L. (2009, March 1). Michelle Obama: Leading lady. *Vogue*. Retrieved from http://www.vogue.com/article/michelle-obama-leading-lady

The Root Staff (2013, February, 5). Why White men are obsessed with the First Lady's butt. *The Root*. Retrieved from http://www.theroot.com/why-white-men-are-obsessed-with-the-first-ladys-butt-1790895126

Thomas, A. J., Witherspoon, K. M., & Speight, S. L. (2004). Toward the development of the stereotypic roles for Black women scale. *Journal of Black Psychology, 30*(3), 426–442.

Thornton, M. C. (2010). "He loves strong, intelligent women. They're his Kryptonite:" Michelle Obama, gender, race, and the black press. In D. Cunnigen & M. M. Bruce (Eds.), *Race in the Age of Obama* (pp. 29–53). Emerald Group Publishing Limited.

Toner, R. (2006, October 26). Ad seen as playing to racial fears. Retrieved from http://www.nytimes.com/2006/10/26/us/politics/26tennessee.html

Tucker, D. M. (1971). Miss Ida B. Wells and Memphis Lynching. *Phylon (1960–)*, *32*(2), 112–122.
Tyson, T. B. (2017). *The Blood of Emmett Till*. New York: Simon and Schuster.
Vontress, C. E. (1971). The Black male personality. *The Black Scholar*, *2*(10), 10–16.
West, C. M. (1995). Mammy, Sapphire, and Jezebel: Historical images of Black women and their implications for psychotherapy. *Psychotherapy: Theory, Research, Practice, Training*, *32*(3), 458.
Wiegman, R. (1993). The anatomy of lynching. *Journal of the History of Sexuality*, *3*(3), 445–467.
Wingfield, A. H. (2007). The modern mammy and the angry Black man: African American professionals' experiences with gendered racism in the workplace. *Race, Gender & Class*, 196–212.
Winter, N. J. G. (2010). Masculine republicans and feminine democrats: Gender and Americans' explicit and implicit images of the political parties. *Political Behavior*, *32*, 587–618. DOI: 1007/s 11109-0189131-z
Yancy, G. (2016). *Black Bodies, White Gazes: The Continuing Significance of Race in America*. Lanham, MD: Rowman & Littlefield.

3

How Obama's Hybridity Stifled Black Nationalist Rhetorical Identity

An Ideological Analysis on His Two-Term Third-Space Leadership

OMOWALE T. ELSON

Contextually, though paradoxically, the economic space between Blacks and Whites perceptually grew wider since Barack Obama's presidency (Blow, 2009), though that phenomenon was trending before he took office in 2008. A signaled event for his Black Nationalists critics was that many Black people lost their homes, a fact that a HUD report attributed to bad lending practices, a lack of equity in people's homes, and the inability to meet monthly repayments as they lost their jobs. The report contended that delinquency was triggered largely "due to a change in their financial circumstances that makes them no longer able to meet their monthly mortgage obligations" (p. 7).

Yet, this bemoaned advantage taken of Black folks who wanted to enter into a middle-class life formed an essential part of the Black Nationalist rhetoric toward the President's inability to address concerns of the Black community. Herein plays out the dissonance of joining or understanding what Obama's racial and cultural identity—being Black and White—really represented. The sociolinguistic tussle for Black Nationalist rhetoric was pegged onto what it meant to hold such a polarity that carried both marginality and power simultaneously—in the sense of which self could be trusted to deliver. Such thinking, of course, would produce an unlikely dissonance because it was constructed in a stereotypical split of allegiance, whereby a visibly forced identification must be made with the marginalized self. In the case of Obama, there could be no bargaining chip, irrespective of the reality that the presidency contained a larger responsibility to others outside of the racial grouping. The dilemma for Black Nationalism, as will be discussed later, is that such bifurcated thinking is limited, archaic, if not destructive in a more globalized world where neo-racism (Lee, 2007) is much more subtle and in which the younger generation is negotiating different ways of leading, responding, and presenting themselves with different kinds of authorized social identities. The question that failed to be pursued is "what can be learned from joining this 'strangeness' that Obama's presidency sprang upon the old guard and contemporary leaders of the Black Nationalist movement?" An attempt will be made to address that question as an epistemological imperative and as an amplification of what is possible when engaging the unknown.

What is explored here are the underlying disruptions in which Obama's hybridity as an ontological and interactional relational concept, unintentionally assaulted the normative Black Nationalist rhetoric that enjoyed a safe camping space in the Black community from which its proponents could rant, feel guilt, shame, include, or exclude the perceived White oppressive majority. At last, it brings Black Nationalist rhetoric under scrutiny for its previously unchallenged notions that it represented an exit strategy for Blacks as a group-as-a-whole out of their perceived oppressed existence (Marable, 1999). In fact, what is argued here is that while the larger platform issue of institutionalized racial discrimination was still a reality facing the Black community in the 21st century in America and elsewhere, the sudden shift in Obama's acquisition of power, and his hybridity, instantaneously became problematic for the Black Nationalist identity trope. The ontological perplexity for Black Nationalism is that it could not address the nature of Black identity without replicating an objectified individual as Obama was made to be. By isolating and castigating his White parts, Obama was made to hold all that is bad and evil, the belittling complex that serves as their raison d'être. In other words, how could Black Nationalists avoid doing to one of their own what White people were doing to them as a group? Choosing a different pathway, the Black elite seemingly seized the opportunity to join the Black President—and like the Congressional Black Caucus not criticize openly—as the preferred followership style on behalf of themselves and the Black community. Cynics labeled this as producing a hypnotic dance that signified the historic pinnacle achievement of Blacks, in the form of

Obama. Reid (2015) captured it succinctly, "For African Americans, the start of the new administration seemed like the beginning of a golden age" (p. 199). It seems that the simple option then was for Obama to be one or the other; he had to be either a certain Black or White, but he was existentially more. Self-preservation staring the Black Nationalists in the face, they would decide for him.

This author believes that relevant to an interrogation of Black Nationalism's stance is to mirror it with a critical ideological perspective, which offers deep insight to examine discursive practices that were premised on values and beliefs about liberation, belonging, progress, and obligation. These values appear as core elements of the Black Nationalist rhetoric that criticized Obama's presidential leadership vis-à-vis the Black community. Indeed, Foss (2009) speaks of ideology as a group's "interpretation of some aspect(s) of the world . . . reflect(s) a group's fundamental social, economic, political, or cultural interests . . . the language . . . a group deploys to make sense of and defines the world or some aspect of it" (p. 209). Elsewhere, Berger (2014) argues that ideological criticism helps people to discover the hidden messages in "mediated and other forms of communication" that shape the way people think about things, events, and other people (p. 106). To that extent, ideology provides a prescripted way of not only defining one's relationship to others and the world, in this case, it becomes an emotional nerve to respond to perceived threats to the in-group, but it also justifies its own existence. Further, if Obama's presidency had signaled the presence of entering into a post-racial society, ideological criticism would look to the traditional structures of intergroup relatedness to determine whether greater symmetrical structures in the socioeconomic public sphere were evident because that would be a marker of a significant shift in authorization. One also might look to Reid's (2015) treatment of "post-racial" in President Obama's authorization of Valerie Jarrett, his senior advisor, to respond to those constituency groups, other than Blacks, who elected him. There, interestingly enough, she implied that traditional Black leadership was kept out of the President's space because many of them had committed their loyalties to the Clintons.

What follows now is a brief review of Black Nationalism's platform and associated statements that appeared in various media and public fora relating to Obama's two terms. Inclusive is an examination of the complexity of the narrative of hybridity that covertly plagues the Black community and the idea of Black unity, but which serves as a background issue of Black Nationalist rhetoric. For one, an exploration of unconscious ways in which the Black community, theorized as a group-as-a-whole (Wells, 1990), communicates its identification and ambivalence through the proponents of Black Nationalist rhetoric, has several associated factors not always evident—social class is one of them. According to Wells (1990), when one person from the group speaks, it frees others to speak on other issues. To that extent, it might appear that the Black Nationalists' constituency, though a relatively small group, exhibits a tacit awareness that as a group it serves to speak of uncomfortable issues that all members of the Black community are unable to articulate in the public domain. The Black Nationalists chose Black poverty for President Obama to address. However, many leaders of this movement are college-level educated and have access to higher standards of living than the masses for whom they speak. Additionally, Obama's presidency did not mean more power to the Black leadership, many of whom were not senators. Furthermore, it is often opaque and thus difficult to magnify the presence of hybridity and its concomitant third-space leadership, which will be explicated later in the chapter. However, it could serve as a new way of articulating a recodification of a progressive Black empowerment discourse. Perhaps some alienation was felt as this nuanced leadership shift was being exemplified through a new Black authorization that Obama skillfully negotiated for a small group of talented Black leaders such as Attorney General Eric Holder and United Nations Ambassador Susan Rice. These authorizations were made under the still hostile gaze of Black Nationalism on one hand, and White supremacy and patriarchal domination on the other. The two latter elements conflate to reproduce an ethic of domination in which Mills (1997) deemed to be a "racial contract" that explains the actual genesis of American society, which perpetuates an "immoral government" that supervises an "unjust" and "exploitative society" through an "immoral code" (p. 5). The structures of the public sphere mentioned earlier would significantly include the holders of supreme power and that would be reflected in the branches of government—Executive, Legislative, and the Supreme Court as well as state apparatuses, all of them designed to oversee inequitable access to resources among different ethnic and socioeconomic groups.

While Black Nationalism and hybridity create a parley that is central to this critique, the intersection of two other background issues—globalization and international identity—manifest within the existence of an implicit spiral that oscillates and illuminates further complexities not readily contemplated within the galactic universe of cultural meaning. This criticism does not idealize a post-racial society that would be embraced by a liberal view; rather, it opens new ways of viewing the deconstruction of race relations where Black leadership is authorized. The question is: for what purpose? And to what extent does this authorization exit? It seems almost scandalously paradoxical to mention a post-racial society and neo-racism in the same breath.

Black Nationalism as Ideology

As a political ideology, Black Nationalism is seen more as an emotional and radical reaction to Black oppression, its rhetorical purpose as a subset of Black rhetoric, is a persuasive campaign directed at White power holders to alter the status quo more equitably (Golden & Rieke, 1995). Some Black scholars dubbed it as lacking pragmatic reach to all sectors of the Black community, especially the professional and managerial class, many of whom were certificated with technical and college degrees (Manning, 1999). Lewis (2000) linked Black Nationalism in the Caribbean to Marcus Garvey's international movement for repatriation of Blacks back to Africa and noted that its central tenants of racial pride and self-determination sought to validate Black masculinity in the face of the White establishment's aim to infantilize Black men as incompetent to assume leadership of the British colonies. While this parallels with the American context, this nationalism was also restricted in its scope for male leadership and the fact that Black was not a nation. Others likened it to White supremacists' tenants of separation and purity of White genes. Therefore, like others, Manning contended that the platform from which many of its proponents spoke out against social injustices and economic disparities were deemed suspect as "anachronistic and self-serving." He noted:

> Their failure to develop a body of politics that takes a qualitative step beyond the discourse and strategies of the Civil Rights Movement of a generation ago is directly linked to the poverty of their theoretical outlook. (p. 151)

It is noteworthy that Davis and Brown (2002) did not qualify Black Nationalism as a theory, but rather as a belief system. Their extensive research on Black Nationalism pointed to two dimensions that define it, community nationalism and separatist nationalism, with its more sustainable and organizationally recognized advocate to be the Nation of Islam, which enunciates its core tenants of "self-determination, racial intolerance, and racial separatism" (p. 241). What was also poignant in these finding was the variance in support among African-American demographics for Black Nationalism. Increases in formal education tended to give one a stake in the power structure and therefore less affinity to this oppositional discourse, at least publicly, and African-American females as a result of perceiving themselves as less a threat formed cross-racial connections, thereby weakening the appeal of Black Nationalism. Consistent with earlier critique, they also found that greater support for "a Black Nationalist belief system leads to greater antipathy toward Whites" (p. 247).

What is important in understanding Black Nationalism's stance toward Obama's presidency is understanding Manning's status as an elevated intellectual in the African-American community. He reportedly lent support to the spirit of the Black Radical Congress that met in Chicago in 1997 with the aim to create a model for making "radical" Black rhetoric relevant. If that were true, it was consistent with the intellectual class's need for a strong theoretical base that would provide practical ways of moving Blacks forward. According to Muwakkil (1998), the Chicago congress put forward 11 "principles of unity" that included, inter alia

- We recognize the diverse historical tendencies in the black radical tradition including revolutionary nationalism, feminism, and socialism.
- Gender and sexuality can no longer be viewed solely as personal issues but must be a basic part of our analysis, politics, and struggles.
- We reject radical and biological determinism, black patriarchy and black capitalism as solutions to problems facing black people.
- We must overcome divisions within the black radical forces such as those of generation, region, and occupation.
- We must forge a common language that is accessible and relevant. (p. 15)

It is significant that in spite of the aforementioned goals, Ards (1998), in a review of the Congress, offered a major critique that the "discussions seem disconnected from the everyday realities of the people we're fighting for" (p. 22). This event followed the Million Men March (MMM), and the Million Women March, both events that targeted the Black community to show unity and commitment to the collective struggle. They were not without intra-group criticism about the respective purposes but, notably, a Black feminist critique was that the MMM was patriarchal in focus. Yet, Ards (1998) opined that the question of how to tap mass energy to fulfill the promises of those events and earlier struggles remains unanswered.

A mere ten years ahead of Obama's election to the presidency, he was not even a blip on the radar of the radical Black agenda of what was possible for Black elevation, even though the issues he engaged as a community organizer represented where radicals were seemingly failing per Manning's critique. The Congress's platform projected an end to the exploitation of capitalism and White racism, injustice in the legal system, and denigration of clean and healthy environments where Black people resided. These large concerns of separatist desire and radical empowerment within the dominant White-controlled United States have long been characterized as Black Nationalism (Ards, 1998; Marable, 1999; Mudimbe 1988 as cited in Germaine (2013); Muwakkil, 2000 & 1998; Price (2009). Perhaps, it is Price's (2009) more recent description of Black Nationalism that puts in context the stance toward Obama's presidency.

> Black Nationalism included . . . support for black self-determination through control of homogenous black institutions, support for black economic and social independence in the form of self-help programs, psychological and social disentanglement from whites and white supremacist notions of black inferiority, and support for a global or Pan-African view of the black community. (Price, 2009, p. 4)

While Black Nationalism champions an economic and political agenda, at times it is difficult to differentiate it from Pan-Africanism, which enunciates unity for Africans in the Diaspora and in Africa, reparations, Black identity, race pride, love of the African features as espoused by Marcus Garvey, and the personification of Black scholarship in the likes of W. E. B. Du Bois and C. L. R. James (Esedebe, 1982). It is from this assumption of who qualifies as Black that so-called progressive public intellectuals would find cause to critique whether Obama was truly Black enough, or understood the needs of Black people who largely looked like him and who helped to secure his election. According to Bialik (2009), writing in the *Wall Street Journal*, Obama captured 95% of the Black vote in 2008 and 93% in 2012 (Pew Research Center, 2012). Incidentally, it should be noted that both reports showed that his overall success in the election and reelection was due to large support from other minorities and young White voters.

Nevertheless, the optics of White technocrats and an elite circle of advisors—several of whom were recruited from corporate America, Clinton's circle, Chicago, and Harvard University, his alma mater, the pinnacle of intellectualism—that surrounded the Black President presented the right mix to cement a link between Black Nationalist and Pan-Africanist rhetoric to render him "not Black enough." The now infamous remarks by Rev. Jesse Jackson that Obama was "talking down to Black people" (CNN, 2008) and Dr. Cornel West's dubbing Obama as the "first Niggerized Black President" (CNN, 2015) would be manifestations of what the Black Nationalist rhetoric has internalized about its own oppression. Mirrored as it is, White Republican conservative leaders in Congress dubbed Obama as the "worst president in the US history," as an ongoing chorus framed to nullify his (Black) authority in the minds of the American people.

That conservative onslaught was coupled with the "birther movement" in alliance with Fox News, which embraced birther proponents from 2011 to 2016, who questioned Obama's claim to U.S. citizenship and, hence, to the presidency (Calderone, 2016). Arguably, this assertion made about Obama's authenticity and competence took a larger presence in the public sphere to the point where he was forced to produce his birth certificate. Black "progressives" serving as opinion leaders, sought to solidify a similar impression in the psyche of the Black community, without the understanding that their own authority would be summarily undermined. Prophetic attention might be gauged from Sean Posey's (2013) analysis in the Hampton Institute:

> It's unclear what impact the disappointing Obama legacy will have for the future of black politics. Still, regardless of whether a Democrat or a Republican occupies the White House in 2017, it's doubtful any agenda addressing black communities will be discussed, much less enacted. In the months and years ahead, it is possible that we will see the rebirth of a new, almost certainly unique and unexpected version of Black Nationalism. (para. 27)

Hybridity

More complex than Black Nationalism is the issue of hybridity, a subject which Obama himself broached during his launch of his book, *Dreams from My Father* (Obama, 1995). As a nexus between two identities with a shared biological connection and co-cultural dialectic, a hybrid identity holds both sides of the tension and more. In fact, the *Guardian*'s writer, Young (2007) noted:

> His mixed-race heritage and solid mid-western timbre have left some claiming he is not black at all. His background—raised

by his white mother and grandparents in Hawaii and Jakarta, he attended Ivy League colleges and then taught constitutional law at university—fits no known mould of black American life. (para. 2)

It is a fact that Obama is bi-racial, bi-national, and co-cultural having a Black Kenyan father and White American mother, and he identifies as Black and Christian. His Muslim education in Indonesia and his Muslim name, at which the Far-Right movement took aim, and which might also have been problematic for the Christian Black community, and his own sense of experiential identity, serve to indicate that this was indeed a complex person. He carried multiple cosmologies that provided nontraditional ways of viewing the world. Indeed, his birth in Hawaii, a colonized island that became the 50th state of the United States did not enhance his American legitimacy. Yet, this issue of hybridity (mixed race/trans-ethnicity) becomes more troublesome as it reflects a dimension of power that previously was unavailable to the African-American or the Black experience before Obama's meteoric rise to the presidency of perceivably the most powerful country in the world. Some would argue that this phenomenon of mixed group embeddedness is not peculiar to African Americans, though it is an exceptional characteristic that catapulted him from a marginalized ethnic minority to lead the majority group that previously stilted the possibilities of his marginalized identities. Within the space of intersectionality then, a hybrid experience would facilitate the construction of a new language, a new discourse, a shifting narrative about more power residing not in the one or other, but in the space between that connects the two original oppositional forces—Black and White. This *third space*, as it were, creates its own leadership (Green & Elson, 2011) and communicative agency that challenges old normative notions of being in the world (Elson, 2007). To that extent, this third-space leadership operates in the "pregnant space," if you will, in which it constantly negotiates a contextually based identity that rejects "my" and "your" space for the option of "our" space, thus moving the whole toward a more altruistic ethic. Case in point: Obama in his acceptance speech in 2009 was hard to locate through the Black Nationalist frame since he raised a broader gender issue as part of the Black experience without using the word "Black" and it went over West's head in his response to the speech. Essentially, this type of leadership has a critical awareness of the forces that privilege one discourse over the other, while being cognizant that historical institutional forces—neocolonialism and White Supremacy—are the greatest of them. It is this fluidity, this uncertain and complex matrix that gives birth to more because hybridity is more than the two separate identities that carry the collective unconscious of a brutalized existence. Unlike the categorization of being Black or White, hybridity then imposes a dynamic and fluid presence that is not easily defined nor held constant. Black Nationalism is brought face-to-face with the age-old tension of skin colorism that plagues the Black community, but it avoids it. It is not new that traditional hybridity (that produces bi-racial individuals) carries greater privilege and is therefore problematic within intragroup racial theorizing of its relative power. It also carries grief. Rape by the White male was implied. Obama had a White mother, and she was not raped. For darker skinned Blacks, the lighter-skinned Blacks truncate their ability to escape the drudgery of aberration, to be chosen over. For light-skinned Blacks, it creates a feeling of isolation from both Black and White groups. Small wonder some outspoken Black public intellectuals hauled Obama over the coals with relative impunity. He also carried the envy, perhaps, of a White mother on one side and the anger on the other side presented a "bad" model for intergroup unification. These are constitutive issues that are not usually addressed in Black Nationalists' discourse, not because they are tabooed, but because they are more reserved for intellectual theorizing.

Russell, Wilson, and Hall (1993) offer a more extensive analysis of this psychological bridging mechanism where, historically, light-skinned Blacks "separated" themselves from dark-skinned Blacks to secure power in the majority population while maintaining a quasi-connection as perceived in the disproportional representation of high-status leadership positions in the Black and majority populations. As an intragroup dynamic, one can argue that light skin carries envy and suspicion, even if and when the best interests of dark-skinned Blacks, whom they represent, are evidently not taken for granted. This was perhaps a dilemma for Obama's seemingly third-space leadership, which had to cultivate a discursive strategy that did not alienate that part of the hybrid identity that was traditionally marginalized. Herein arises a complex navigational territory that Obama's presidency confronted at the boundary of Black Nationalist discourse. It was fixed! Race as identity, notes Steele (1990) in his book *The Content of our Character: A New Vision of Race in America*, was "pressed into service in a social and political war against oppression" (p. 100). One might infer then that Obama's dark-skinned wife, Michelle, who served as his professional mentor in a law firm, later activated that socializing role by "embedding" him spiritually into a Black church, in which his Blackness could be legitimized. Unfortunately, he was forced to abandon the Black church in order to secure the presidency, and to distance himself from the main tenants of the Black Nationalist agenda as espoused by his pastor, Rev.

Jeremiah Wright, Jr. (Kantor, 2007). From the group-as-a-whole perspective, Rev. Wright had articulated an uncomfortable relationship dynamic on behalf of the Black community, which Obama was supposed to make part of his presidential platform. But at last, it presented a fault-line that tested his Black alliance. The Reverend Wright controversy then served as the signal point on how Obama's hybridity further stifled the traditional Black Nationalist rhetoric by bringing it under the jaundiced microscope of national (media) attention.

At least for Black Nationalists, the high dreaming of hope and the high expectations of disappointment converged in the co-constructed space that characterized what was old and deficient with what was new and confounding about the new third-space leadership the President was offering. For them, it might have confirmed that they would have to stay the course because his presidency made no difference to their radical cause. This position confirmed Manning's critique mentioned earlier of Black Nationalism's lack of theoretical grounding.

Convergence Spiral

What is being talked about summarily and presented hereafter is a model that highlights a constellation of evolving and nuanced relationships that are central to the explication of a critique of Black Nationalism's impact on Obama's presidency in the two terms, see Figure 3.1. It is more than an info-graph that depicts key elements that characterize the subheadings—globalization, Black Nationalism, transnationalism, and hybridity. Figure 3.1 is also a dynamic convergence spiral of conscious and unconscious interactions that are communicated through contexts—shared ambivalences and vulnerabilities—that served as background influences to how messages are encoded and framed about Black people, but for which Black Nationalism is not considered as displayed in this composite form. Part of the complexity is that the rhetorical strategy of invective targeting a White enemy gets confused when it merges with other identities, especially their own.

An apparent significance of the spiral complex is that it contains the time and scale elements such as movement within and across identities and belongingness as exemplified in the Black Nationalist literature and discussion above. Importantly too, it highlights a typology that falls out from the four key interactional background environments—nationalism, hybridity, globalization, and transnationalism—that are essentially convergent cohabiters rather than polar opposites. Hence, it recognizes that Black Nationalism as an ideological critique for Obama's presidency would

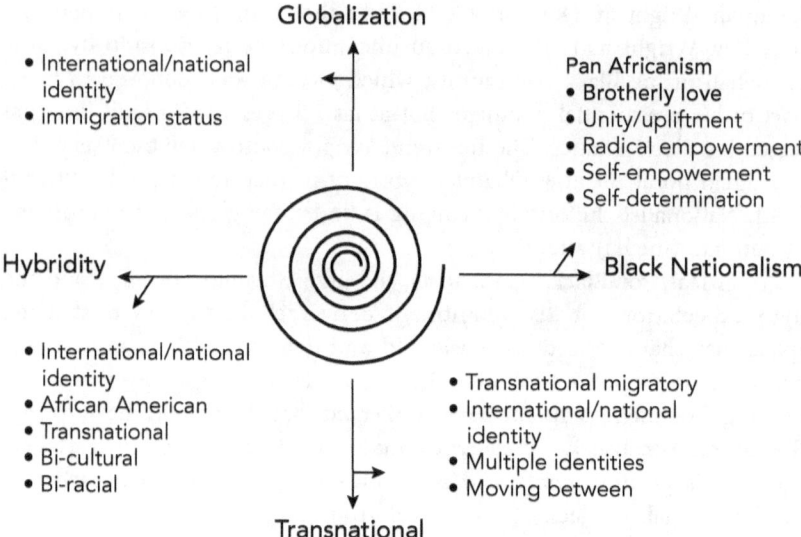

Figure 3.1. Convergence Spiral of Identity Complex for Black Nationalism.

need to be revised, if only because Black Nationalism essentially bifurcates and simplifies these complexities to rationalize a separate existence, a false hope.

Black Nationalism Misreads the Context

From the analysis so far, it becomes evident that Black Nationalism has limited scope in transforming the objective economic conditions of the larger Black population in the United States for which it seemingly advocates. Paradoxically, this lack is the precise issue for which they criticized President Obama. It appears that, while its historical function was to serve as an alarm against extreme neo-colonial brutality and acts of humiliation as evidenced in contemporary Black community-police relations, in educational and employment disparities, and in wealth ownership, Black Nationalism misinterpreted its purpose vis-à-vis Obama's presidency. From the start, Black Nationalist discourse, reflecting its core, sought to treat the Obama's presidency as its traditional enemy. It stressed that he would be held accountable as if this emanated from a consultation with the Black community. This raised questions about the implications of this self-appointed mission. A reasonable inference is that by pursuing that path, Obama's Blackness would be rendered invisible so that a clear shot at his Whiteness would be unimpeded. This is typified in the statements below of his being "half-Black." Mirroring this fantasy was the reminder that Obama was raised White by his White mother and White grandparents, which would be a cultural rather than a racial argument, given they were silent on the fact that his father was a Black African from Kenya. Consequently, either intentionally or unintentionally, such a strategy eventually would render them helpless and totally inept. For the first time, the Black Nationalist rhetoric in juxtaposition with far-right and White Nationalist movements—White supremacy—crystalized into a similarity. The tragedy, however, is that this Nationalists' stance was shortsighted; it seemingly glorified the narrative of marginalization and victimology, and of being ignored or left behind. Of course, it was a rhetorical strategy that worked well against previous presidents, all of whom were White and male. One could argue that the inability to explore whether Obama's White enculturation might be experienced as a different Whiteness given its Hawaiian influence, or that his hybridity might mean a more empowered Blackness, is theoretical, if not the ethical dilemma of Black Nationalism. It is not a small factor that he is married to a dark-skinned woman, who mentored him professionally and whom he trusted. It could not be that the chief spokespersons of Black Nationalism had an inability to learn the transitional language that hybridity engendered. It could not be that they had difficulty recognizing this co-cultural, bi-racial dynamic. It could not be that they did not have an interest in gaining new ground and consolidating new achievements. No, the answer is not blowing somewhere in the wind!

One can proffer an identity crisis of massive proportion for the Black Nationalists. In the two terms of Obama's presidency, Black Nationalism was actually displaying an inability to abandon its tactic of vilification to differentiate what kind of White was a problem, and what type of Black could be authorized on its behalf. Is it possible that Obama was signaling that here is a group of White folks that I worked with in building an alliance for transformation after my two terms end? Inevitably, and unconsciously, Black Nationalism was siding with White Nationalist right-wingers and "birthers" who conversely were working to render Obama's Whiteness invisible, his Blackness useless and despicable, and his humanity and competence, which are tied to his Blackness, well, highly intolerable and inconsequential. At no moment did the Black Nationalists claim enough power to say to the Far-Right, not so fast on this one, we got the Black President's back. The small group of Blacks on the left who did was immediately cast as his "stooges," a charge leveled at Black TV's sociopolitical commentators, including Melissa Harris-Perry, Van Jones, Roland Martin, and Ta-Nehisi Coates.

Intel from the Field

Google searches of social media and online (popular) publications using key terms that were coupled with Obama and his antagonists—Cornel West, Tavis Smiley, and a number of Republicans, namely Mitch McConnell, Glenn Beck, Donald Trump, Rush Limbaugh, Jerry Falwell, etc.—yielded an amazing typology/taxonomy that characterizes attempts to render invisible Obama's Blackness, and Blackness as incompetence. Invisibility represents a stripping away of one's physical and cultural artifacts until homogeneity replaces differentiation, see Figure 3.2: Media-Generated Perceptions of Obama.

In this taxonomy, the labeling tactics were similar, noted examples included such invectives as "Some sorta Black president" or "half-Black President." The difference, of course, was that neither Republicans nor the Far-Right had the license to reference the "niggerized" assault, perhaps the lowest gut attack imagined, on President Obama. Think that Obama–Black Nationalist tension reflected an intragroup conflict?

What is clear from this captured discourse in figure 3.2 is that the resentment for President Obama, as evidenced in one of the prominent Black Nationalists' spokesmen, Dr. Cornel West, and the Far-Right narratives, is that these unlikely adversarial pairs become bedfellows in pursuit of a common enemy. It should be noted that those comments included in figure 3.2 are those that reflected ad hominem attacks and not those directed at the Office of the President; they signified something deeply personal and, at once, extreme. Take for example West's comment of a "niggerized" President. That comment stands to affirm the Far-Right's stereotypical belief of the inadequacy of Black leadership and the right to achieve such high political authority. The convergence of these hostilities might be better understood through Wells's (1998) conceptualization of transubstantiation error, the act of transforming the culture of another group into one's own epistemology or system of knowing the world (pp. 406–408). He argues that this process can also reflect ethnocentrism in that the unconscious goal is to protect or defend the in-group's sense of superiority while it devalues and maligns the out-group. So then one might reasonably accept that, for Black Nationalism, President Obama was an outsider to the Black community. On the other side of this argument is the problem it poses for conceptualizing a post-racial society when race

Black Nationalists comments	Republicans comments	Far Right comments
- "First Niggerized Black President" (West, CNN, 2008) - "Some sorta Black president" - "half-black president" - "spineless" - "milquetoast" for kowtowing to corporate interests - "the black mascot of Wall Street oligarchs." (May 2011 interview with Truthdig) - "Most comfortable with upper-middle-class white and Jewish men who consider themselves very smart." (Cornell West) - "I wanted to slap him on the side of his head." - "A Republican, a Rockefeller Republican in blackface." - "All he has known culturally is white . . . When he meets an independent black brother, it is frightening." - "Obama, coming out of Kansas influence, white, loving grandparents, coming out of Hawaii and Indonesia, when he meets these independent black folk who have a history of slavery, Jim Crow, Jane Crow and so on, he is very apprehensive." - "He has a certain rootlessness, a deracination. It is understandable." - http://nymag.com/news/features/cornel-west-2012-5/) (Truthdig) - (Cornel West) (November 2012 interview with Democracy Now) (https://www.washingtonpost.com/blogs/post-partisan/wp/2016/01/22/how-cornel-west-hurts-bernie-sanders/)	- "the worst president we've ever had." (Cheney, 2015) Huffington Post (http://wegoted.com/2015/04/cheney-calls-president-obama-the-worst-president-we-have-ever-had/) - "worst President in America's history." (Trump, www.cnn.com/2016/02) - "Our great African American President hasn't exactly had a positive impact on the thugs who are so happily and openly destroying Baltimore!" (Trump, 28 Apr 2015) - "He has done such a lousy job as president." (Trump) - "a threat to our country." (Trump, wtvr.com/.Nov 19, 2015)	- race-baiter-in-chief (http://www.slate.com/articles/news_and_politics/politics/2016/05/donald_trump_is_everything_the_right_wing_made_barack_obama_out_to_be.html) - Simply does not understand what it means to be president. (http://www.slate.com/articles/news_and_politics/politics/2016/05/donald_trump_is_everything_the_right_wing_made_barack_obama_out_to_be.html)

Figure 3.2. Media-Generated Perceptions of Obama.

or racialization (Balibar, 2007) is deeply embedded in the collective consciousness of the White, Black, and Brown communities or, as President Obama said in a radio interview with Marc Macon (NPR, 2015), racism is deeply institutionalized and casts a long shadow.

One might wonder whether splitting Whiteness from Blackness or vice versa is a healthy undertaking given that at a deeply personal level it is the individual whose claims of identity must be respected. Internationally renowned golfer, Tiger Woods, navigated this experience. On a rational plain, one would expect that a person who is allowed to claim all of his or her identity parts would be more present than a fragmented person. So, herein steps hybridity as a sociocultural concept that adds further complexity. When the world is viewed as Black and White, the issues seem to beg for reductionist positions of what Germain (2013) called the "new Black Nationalism," wherein Black Nationalists perceive declining identities that can be merged and perhaps obliterated. For example, increasing interracial marriages could be perceived as a threat to Blackness. In this line of reasoning, it might be better to keep Blackness separated from Whiteness since, historically, combining them has at times been hurtful or misunderstood. This represents a big discursive shift for Black Nationalism, which has avoided the prickly issue of skin colorism in the Black community. West's reference to Obama as a "Rockefeller Republican in blackface," above speaks to the difficulty of Black Nationalism to accept Obama's hybridity as a whole. It might also represent West's splitting of his discomfort given the prima facie evidence of light-skinned privilege accorded to his Black Nationalist role.

Whither a New Black Leadership

A critique on Black Nationalism vis-à-vis Obama's presidency is partly a questioning of the radical Black leadership discursive function and its inability to authorize a Black man in a role that was not previously imaginable for him to occupy. The task of dealing with an incoherent movement driven by values of victimology seems no longer tenable. Obama's elevation would appear to be one of those moments of steroid change that was too swift for consensus reality (Mindell, 2010) to comprehend its historical implication. To normalize such swiftness that leaped over 300 years of impossibility would require a new lexicon to enunciate what was now possible, even though objective conditions of racial equity remain an incomplete project. What it would mean for Black Nationalists to embrace an office that was previously alien to the high dreams of Black people might be answered through a strong theoretical disposition, that is, premised on tested negotiated principles that have been employed with historical reflection and contemporary success, partly gleaned from Obama's tenure as a two-term president. Such principles and values would have to be based on a fierce ethics of common cause-benefit that transcend narrow definitions of social identity. One might ask where in the Black experience this has happened. There might be more evidence to point to a lack since little effort was made to continue the collaborative work across racial lines that was possible in the later years of Malcolm X, Martin Luther King Jr., Shirley Chisholm, or Barbara Jordan as notable historical figures. One might perceive Obama's legacy as a larger gain in moving the race needle.

To have made such a forward movement, to embrace Obama as Black and more than Black, Black Nationalists would have had to cease holding as constant the idea of oppressed Black people as a fixed, lived reality that cannot be truly transformed, not even through the symbolization of the hybridity that Obama signifies—not only as racial, but as common-cause-benefit that regards equal citizenship, shared social and economic distribution of the wealth as well as through the opportunity to desire, dream, create, and innovate a new generational future. In order for that dreaming to be legitimized, the White part of Obama would have to be synchronized with his Black identity parts, not over and above them, as suggested in figure 3.2. Resultantly, the unconsciously fixed, long-cultivated, and battle-tried identity of the Black Nationalist persona would face diminishment or worse, annihilation. One could argue that the lack of support for Obama's presidency was due in large part to a Black Nationalist situational crisis—they could not offend the larger sector of the Black community who supported him, while they pandered to a small vocal base. It might also mean that shifts in racial relations and accomplishments in business, science, entertainment, sports, education, and politics are not genuinely embraced as a movement toward a post-racial society but rather a reflection of an unveiled neo-race society.

Public scholars like Cornell West at some visceral level might have some cognitive processing that with Obama's election the race narrative had shifted given the increased interracial interactions and unions (Wang, 2012). The reason why West and others of his ilk were unable to acknowledge it begs the question. This is not a simple issue. In looking at the group-as-a-whole perspective, at the individual level of analysis, one would find that the individual's cognitive reflections form the essential image that the person carries of himself or herself as a member of a particular group. It might be that the last bastion of oppression to overcome in the group-as-a-whole view would be at the institutional level of analysis where traditional authority has been White and male. Even though the self might become a mirror image of a projected assessment from another group and this forms an essential sine qua non of the group's existential navigation into the cultural terrain that is hostile and friendly, conscious and unconscious, rational and irrational, it is also highly unpredictable and unstable in its expectations of accommodating a Black person at the top. This essentially is Black Nationalism's quandary because it does not offer support for maintaining and achieving such institutional leadership from which its goals can be achieved, at least not as they are conceptualized.

It took former presidential candidate Senator Bernie Sanders, who West had embraced, to explain that it does not matter who is elected president, that person could not succeed with a radical agenda without the mass support of a strongly mobilized movement. Besides, mainstream media commentators from the supposed left formed a consensus that President Obama was under racist assault from a Republican-controlled Congress for his leftist policies such as Obamacare, LBGTQ rights, dreamers, free college education, and minimum wage. Seemingly, to accept this understanding of how the American political system works, which everyone rationally knows, would require Black Nationalism to revisit its traditional rhetoric given that a Black man occupied its favorite targeted power position and another minority might follow suit.

I would like to acknowledge the input of Dr. John L. Johnson who offered perspectives on the group-as-a-whole theorizing and for materials he shared from his private library on Black Nationalism.

References

Ards, A. (1998). *The new Black radicalism.* New York: *The Nation*.

Balibar, E. (2007). Is there a 'Neo-Racism'? In T. Gupta, R. Maak, G. Galabuzi & C. Andersen (Eds.). Toronto: Canadian Scholars' Press.

Berger, A. (2014). *Media and communication research methods: An introduction to qualitative and quantitative approach.* (3rd ed.). San Francisco: Sage.

Bialik, C. (2009). Did race win the election for Obama? Retrieved February 8, 2015, from www.wsj.com.

Blow, C. (2009). Black in the Age of Obama. Retrieved from: http://www.nytimes.com/2009/12/05/opinion/05blow.htm

Calderone, M. (2016). Fox News gives Donald Trump a pass on Birther Crusade it helped fuel. Retrieved on May 15, 2017, from http://www.huffingtonpost.com/entry/fox-news-donald-trump-birtherism_us_57e54a06e4b08d73b830d54e

Davis, D., & Brown, R. (2002). The antipathy of Black Nationalism: Behavioral and attitudinal implications of an African American ideology. *American Journal of Political Science, 46*(2), 239–252.

Democracy Now (2009). Cornel West on the Election of Barack Obama: "I Hope He Is a Progressive Lincoln, I Aspire to Be the Frederick Douglass to Put Pressure on Him." Retrieved on December 19 from https://www.democracynow.org/2008/11/19/cornel_west_on_the_election_of

Elson, O. (2007). Gender-Agency as communication in the intro-interorganizational structures of the Spiritual Baptist of Barbados: A postcolonial account of cultural resistance. *Howard Journal of Communication, 18*(1), 15–37.

Esedebe, P. O. (1982). *Pan-Africanism: The idea and movement—1776–1963*. Washington, DC: Howard University Press.

Foss, S. (2009). *Rhetorical criticism: Exploration and practice.* (4th ed.). Long Grove, IL: Waveland Press.

Germaine, F. (2014). A "new" Black Nationalism in the USA bad France. *Journal of African American Studies, 18*, 286–304.

Golden, J., & Rieke, R. (1995). Black rhetoric. In L. A. Niles (Ed.), *African American Rhetoric: A Reader.* Dubuque, IA: Kendall/Hunt Publishing Company.

Green Z., & Elson, O. (2012). Unleashing possibilities: Leadership and the third space. In Carol Pearson (Ed.), *The transforming leader: New approaches to leadership for the Twentieth-First Century.* San Francisco: Berrett-Koehler Publishers.

Jackson apologizes for "crude" Obama his remarks. Retrieved on from January 25, 2016, http://www.cnn.com/2008/POLITICS/07/09/jesse.jackson.comment/

Kantor, J. (2007). A candidate, his minister and the search for faith. Retrieved on May 10, from http://www.nytimes.com/2007/04/30/us/politics/30obama.html

Lee, J. (2007). Neo-racism toward international students: A critical need for change. *About Campus, 11*, 28–30.

Lewis, L. (2000). "Nationalism and Caribbean Masculinity." In T. Mayer (Ed.)., *Gender Ironies of Nationalism: Sexing the Nation.* New York and London: Routledge.

Manning, M. (1999). *Black leadership: Four great American leaders and the struggle for Civil Rights.* New York: Penguin Books.

Mills, C. (1997). *The racial contract.* Ithaca, NY: Cornell University Press

Muwakkil, S. (1998). *Black radicalism: Where do we go from here? Developing a left politics for African-Americans.* Chicago: In These Times.

Obama, B. (1995). *Dreams from My Father: A Story of Race and Inheritance.* New York: Three Rivers.

Pew Research Center (2012). Changing face of America helps assure Obama victory. Retrieved on February 9, 2016, from www.people-press.org.

Posey, S. (2013). Will Black Nationalism Reemerge? Hampton Institute. Retrieved on January 20, 2016. http://www.hamptoninstitution.org/blacknationalism.html#.V4AhcNIrLX4

Price, M. (2009). *Dreaming of blackness: Black Nationalism and African American public opinion.* New York: NTU Press.

Reid, J. (2015). *Fracture: Barack Obama, the Clintons, and the racial divide.* Harper Collins Publishers: New York.

Russell, K., Wilson, M., & Hall, R. (1993). *The color complex: politics of skin color among African Americans*. Anchor Book Doubleday: New York

Steele, S. (1990). *The content of our character: A vision of race in America*. New York: Harper Perential.

Young, G. (2007). Is Obama black enough? Retrieved on January 24, 2016, from: http://www.theguardian.com/world/2007/mar/01/usa.uselections2008

Wang, W. (2012). The Rise of Intermarriage. Retrieved from http://www.pewsocial trends.org/2012/02/16/the-rise-of-intermarriage/

Wells, L. (1990). Group-as-a-whole: A systematic socioanalytic perspective on interpersonal and group relations. In J. Gillette & M. McCollom (Ed.), *Groups in context: A new perspective on group dynamics* (pp. 49–85). Boston, MA: Addison-Wesley Publishing Company.

Wells, L. (1998). The effects of ethnicity on the quality of student life: An embedded intergroup analysis. *The Journal of Applied Behavioral Science*, 24, 403–417.

Part II

4

"Who Gets to Say Hussein?

The Impact of Anti-Muslim Sentiment During the Obama Era"

Nura A. Sediqe

On January 20, 2008, when Barack Obama stood to take his oath as the 44th President of the United States, he recited his full name, "I, Barack *Hussein* Obama." There was speculation among Muslims whether he would recite his entire name on stage, and swearing in with a visibly Muslim name was a statement that Muslims in the United States paid close attention to. During the 2007 campaign season, whispers of the name Hussein permeated public discourse and was emphasized as a suspicious element of his identity. It was as if his middle name were a racial slur. Yet Obama's clear enunciation of his full name ushered in enthusiasm amongst Muslims that he was embracing a part of his identity that was under suspicion. Barack Obama's ascension to the Office of the President ushered in shifting racial dynamics that complicated conversations about race in the U.S. With regard to his social identity, the focus was on his Blackness, but Obama's religious identity, by virtue of his name alone, also became connected to that of Muslims in the United States.

This chapter focuses on the climate surrounding the perception and treatment of Muslims and then analyzes how it affected the attitudes of Muslims themselves. The effect of these perceptions on Muslims in the U.S. highlights one emerging manifestation of neo-racism. Another salient example of anti-Muslim sentiment that is arguably neo-racial was the conversation around President Obama himself. Having a Muslim name is one element of Obama's identity that has remained under-examined as well as the consequences of that element of his identity. The aforementioned, in addition to the sociopolitical climate surrounding Islam and Muslims during the Obama era, is investigated in this chapter.

This chapter rests on the assumption that the State is *inherently* racial (Omi and Winant, 1986). Racial meanings are assigned to groups, and in the case of Muslims, the racial meaning, being labeled as a "suspicious, foreign other" was further reified with the election of President Obama in 2008 (Beydoun, 2016; Jamal, 2008). In many ways, the process of racializing Muslims in the U.S. suggests that this is a manifestation of neo-racism. Neo-racism contends that racism, in its contemporary forms, will avoid discourse of biological distinctions and emphasize the incompatibility of lifestyles and traditions. Balibar & Wallerstein (1991) contends that "It is a racism whose dominant theme is not biological heredity but the insurmountability of cultural differences, a racism which, at first sight, does not postulate the superiority of certain groups or peoples in relation to others but 'only' the harmfulness of abolishing frontiers, the incompatibility of life-styles and traditions . . ." (p. 21). In the case of Muslims, neo-racial meanings focus on the difference in religion and culture, which are seen as foreign, suspicious, and often tied to terror-oriented violence. Racialization, specifically, is the process of institutional powers, such as government institutions, ascribing a broad umbrella term and specific meaning on subordinated groups (Omi and Winant, 1994). The tension around Obama's middle name is indicative of how racialized the discourse was during his two terms in office.

Understanding the sociopolitical climate of these external perceptions also introduced the additional dynamic of how Obama's Administration racialized Muslims in the United States. The surveillance of Muslim Americans continued during the Obama administration and placed institutional emphasis on Muslims as a different "enemy-other." Thus, it is ironic that while the Obama Administration's policies continued the racialization of Muslims, President Obama himself was affected by the growing anti-Muslims opinions in the U.S. The "birther movement" is closely tied to these accusations whereby individuals, notably then-businessman Donald Trump, speculated about Obama's birth certificate and asserted that Obama was hiding the fact that he was actually born in Kenya. In 2011, Trump told Fox News, "He doesn't have a birth certificate. He may have one, but there's something on that, maybe religion, maybe it says he is a Muslim . . . I don't know. Maybe he doesn't want that" (Johnson and Hauslohner, 2017). The birther movement's accusations brought such pressure that, in April 2011, President Obama attended the White House briefing room to denounce Trump's accusations (Moody and Holmes, 2015). In the most recent national election survey performed by the American National Election Study in 2016, respondents were asked whether they believed that President Obama was Muslim. As figure 4.1 shows, there is an interesting pattern that emerged along racial lines whereby 33% of White respondents believed that President Obama was Muslim, compared to 11% of Black respondents. This is one manifestation of neo-racism whereby Obama himself was believed to be Muslim, even though his avowed religious identity is Christian.

Public Perceptions and the Obama Administration

In order to understand how emphasizing the word "Hussein" aroused suspicion of Muslims, it is important to identify how the media conversation and public perceptions of Muslims fostered a stereotype of Muslims as being "other." One of the earlier points where Muslims became part of public discourse was with the 1979 revolution in Iran, which was also punctuated by a highly publicized broadcast of the Iranian hostage crisis (Curtis, 2013; Jamal & Naber, 2011). Muslims were pictured as potentially

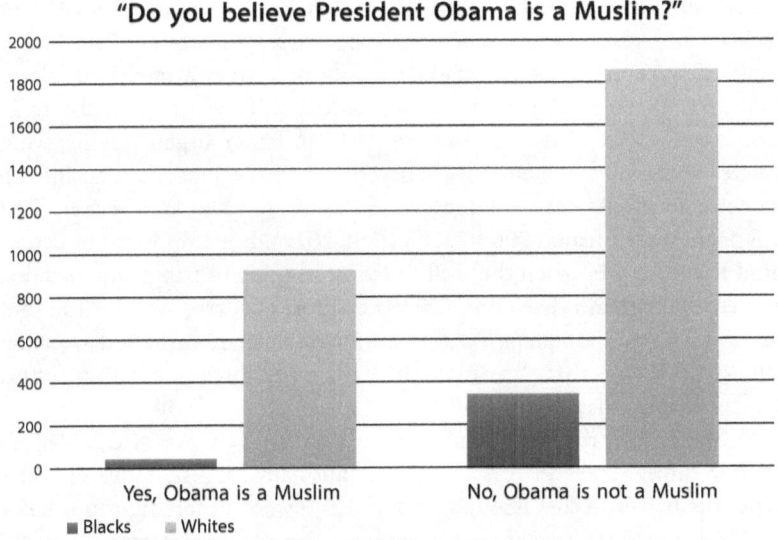

Figure 4.1. "Do You Believe President Obama Is a Muslim?"

dangerous in the midst of this conflict (Curtis 2013). This depiction of Muslims as a national security threat, and foreign outsiders emerged within the discourse around this crisis. It also permeated the film industry with characterizations of Muslims as predominantly associated with a threat to national security, terrorists, and as foreigners. These patterns highlighted how Muslims were and are "racially lumped" together as one collective entity.

While stereotypes around Muslims have existed throughout history during different time periods, the attention toward the Muslim community amplified after the September 11, 2001, attacks (Alsultany, 2012; Esposito & Kalin, 2011; Shaheen, 2015). The perpetrators of these acts who claimed responsibility were individuals who originated from Muslim-majority countries. The discourse within the 24-hour news cycle and print media began bringing Islam as a religious tradition into the conversation. In particular, there was particular focus on the adherents of Islam within the United States (Alsultany, 2008; Joseph et al., 2008).

What made the Obama era unique was the rising prevalence of this discourse that emerged around the time that Senator Barack Obama declared his bid to run for president. While some of the messaging around Muslims as suspicious remained in far-right circles, which shifted over time, far-right activists increased their contention that Muslims, by virtue of their religious tradition, were at odds with American principles of freedom, and argued that incompatible differences existed between Muslims and other individuals in the U.S. (Ali et al., 2011). Organizations with explicitly anti-Muslim mission statements (labeled as "fringe organizations") were tracked, and researchers found that their messages around "Muslims as enemies" were not ones that made it within mainstream media circulation from 2001 through 2003, but then a marked shift occurred in the mainstream press (Bail, 2012). The messages from fringe organizations, which are clear examples of neo-racist discourse, became incorporated into the mainstream media conversation around 2004 to 2006, and became fairly well pronounced from 2006 to 2008 (Bail, 2012). It is important to keep in mind the timing of when the shift in the messaging of fringe organizations entered mainstream discourse. That transition occurred around the same time that Barack Obama's bid for the Democratic nomination occurred. Bail (2012) argues that, ". . . mass media is a key force in creating cultural change during unsettled times" (p. 857).

Figure 4.2 provides public opinion data from the American National Election Study (2008, 2012), whereby a nationally representative sample of respondents were asked about their feelings toward different groups before the 2008 and 2012 presidential elections. The scale went from 0 to 100, with zero referencing "very cold or unfavorable feeling" and 100 referencing "very warm or favorable feeling." The average score for Muslims, in terms of favorability was 43.35 in 2008, and decreased to 40.6 by 2012. There is a 26-point difference between Muslims and Christians, with Christian groups' favorability at 69.6 in 2008 and 66.6 in 2012. Given what is known about the time period, the information presented within this poll helped capture the degree to which there were cold to lukewarm feelings toward Muslims as a group. Interestingly, there was an increase of positive feelings toward Muslims in 2016, near the end of Obama's term in office.

The perceptions of Muslims and the stereotypes that were prevalent are important to keep in mind when assessing the treatment of Muslims during the Obama era, because President Obama himself was subject to the stereotypes associated with Muslims. President Obama's background gave his critics opportunity for much speculation about his loyalties. Obama's father was Kenyan and from a Muslim family. Moreover, Obama spent part of his childhood in Indonesia (a Muslim-majority country), and media brought a frenzy of reports that Obama attended a "madrasa." While President Obama and his family had an active history of attending the Trinity United Church of Christ in Chicago, speculation of being Muslim continued unabated throughout his two terms in office.

One of the most prominent examples in the 2008 presidential campaign run was a broadcast town hall meeting with Republican nominee, John McCain. One audience member turned toward Senator McCain and said, "I can't trust Obama. I have read about him and he's not, he's not uh—he's an Arab. He's not—" before McCain retook the microphone and

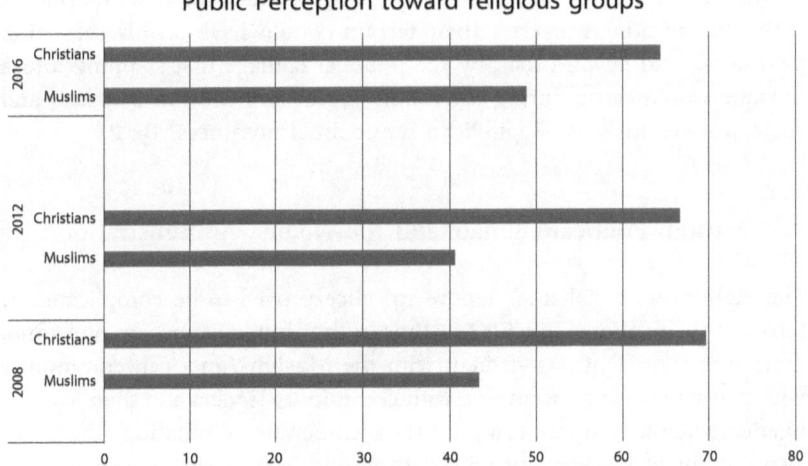

Figure 4.2. Public Perceptions toward Religious Groups.

replied: "No, ma'am. He's a decent family man [and] citizen that I just happen to have disagreements with on fundamental issues and that's what this campaign's all about. He's not [an Arab]" (Martin & Parnes, 2008). The subtlety of McCain's response was not lost on the public or high-ranking Republicans within the party. General Colin Powel (2008), in response, stated, "The correct answer is, he is not a Muslim, he's a Christian. He's always been a Christian," Powell said. "But the *really* right answer is: What if he is? Is there something wrong with being a Muslim in this country? The answer's no. That's not America. Is there something wrong with some seven-year-old Muslim American kid believing that he or she could be president?" (Powel, 2008). General Powel made an important observation in stating, so what if Obama were Muslim. It disrupted the conversation that had occurred around President Obama to identify the deeper issue at hand, what was so wrong with being associated with Muslims? Emphasizing President Obama's middle name, and the use of subtle dismissive remarks like the one that John McCain offered at the town hall helped to reify the perception of Muslims as a suspicious other, and the subtle ways in which it functioned in this specific example demonstrates the ways neo-racism worked within public discourse.

Scholars have speculated that the aforementioned comments and suspicions influenced the distance that Obama kept from the Muslim community (Beydoun, 2016). For example, President Obama did not visit a mosque until, his eighth year in office, which sparked a conversation of, "Why so long?" Legal scholar Khaled Beydoun (2016) argues that, ". . . steering clear from American mosques for seven years was not driven by explicit Islamophobia. But rather, by fear of the personal cost that interfacing with Muslim Americans, on their terrain, would have on his reelection prospects. And beyond that, by the political damage that stepping into a mosque would cause during the rising tide of anti-Muslim backlash and rhetorical venom from Republican presidential nominees" (p. 2).

Muslim Political Climate and the Obama Administration

The eight years of Obama's tenure in office proved to be complicated in terms of the relationship with Muslims in the United States. On one hand, there was consistent engagement with the Muslim-American community with private meetings occurring with community leaders and then Senator Obama when he was still vying for the Democratic nomination. There was also continued engagement with community leaders and advocates such as Senior White House advisers Valerie Jarrett and department heads like

Homeland Security Secretary Janet Napolitano and Attorney General Eric H. Holder Jr., during Obama's tenure as president (Elliott, 2008). Additionally, there were also public actions that demonstrated the administration's more welcoming approach to Muslims. For example, prominent European Muslim academic Tariq Ramadan was banned from entering the United States for an academic appointment at Notre Dame University during the Bush administration's tenure, but Secretary of State Hillary Clinton reversed the decision and Tariq Ramadan was permitted to enter for the first time in six years (Lyall, 2010). There were also active public efforts to engage segments of the Muslim community with annual dinners held at the White House during Ramadan, and public messages that President Obama would convey to commemorate cultural events like the Iranian New Year (Elliot, 2010). In many respects, some members of Muslim communities were optimistic about their relationship with the Obama Administration, and trusted in the President's commitment to keep the interests of Muslims in the U.S. in mind.

On the other hand, the specific government programs that continued during President Obama's time in office suggested that the process of racializing Muslims would continue. The Bush administration ushered in programs like the National Security Entry-Exit Registration System (NSEERS), which registered travelers from predominantly Muslim-majority countries, if they traveled to the United States. Programs such as NSEERS continued during Obama's term as president. Elements of the Patriot Act were renewed, and civil rights groups expressed concern about the continued surveillance of certain communities (Beydoun, 2016; Serwer, 2013). Furthermore, it was during Obama's tenure as president that the Associated Press (2012) revealed that the New York Police Department (NYPD) had established a special investigative unit that participated in a broad surveillance program and mapping of Muslim communities, not only in New York, but within the surrounding region. It was also revealed, for example, that students at NYU and Yale University were among the many that NYPD officials surveilled through this program. The Asian American Legal Defense Fund expressed concerns over the impact of such surveillance, "The program has stifled speech, communal life and religious practice and criminalized a broad segment of American Muslims. The isolationism that comes with being a 'spied on' community means that American Muslims are getting a fundamentally inferior opportunity to exercise their constitutional rights" (AALDEF, 2013, p. 1). For many in Congress, the Obama Administration's response to the news of this program was also telling, as it was lukewarm and delayed. Attorney General Eric Holder had stated that the Department of Justice (DOJ) would investigate the matter, but in 2013, a year after the news was revealed, members of Congress expressed concern about the delay in response from the DOJ and the lack of communication between Congress and the DOJ (Serwer, 2013).

While engagement with Muslim communities occurred during the Obama Administration, it also included the institutionalized profiling and targeting of Muslim Americans through programs such as the one the NYPD had placed within their region. The institutional forces, such as the police department's targeted profiling of Muslims, were not actions limited to the auspices of a Republican Administration, but continued during the Obama's presidency. This profiling by government institutions of Muslims as a "suspicious other" exhibited how the State reinforced a specific meaning on Muslims as foreign, other, and ones to watch—all highlighting one of the most pronounced ways neo-racism affected Muslims during the Obama era.

Who Are Muslim Americans?

If Muslims are not a suspicious other, who are they? And what are the consequences of neo-racism on how Muslims perceive themselves and their collective group identity as Muslims? The Muslim population in the U.S. is estimated to be between 3.1 and 8 million people (CAIR 2016; Pew 2016). Islam is also the fastest growing religion in the United States (Lipka and Hackett, 2015; NPR, 2016). Figure 4.3 highlights the diverse countries of origin that make up Muslims in the U.S., according to the 2011 Pew Survey of Muslims in America.

There are distinct histories among subgroups of Muslims that are important to keep in mind, as this can complicate how individuals approach their sense of holding a collective Muslim group identity. The oldest Muslim communities trace their origins to enslaved Africans brought primarily to the South through the transatlantic slave trade (Curtis, 2005; Diouf, 2013). While the practice of Islam faded from enslaved communities through the generations, the re-emergence of Islam in the United States was in great part due to Black Americans converting to Islam, intentionally connecting their embrace of Islam as a means of reclaiming their ancestral history to Africans (Curtis, 2005; Diouf, 2013). This led to the establishment of various Muslim communities from the Moorish Science Temple to the Nation of Islam. While theologically different from orthodox Islam, adherents of this branch of the tradition were vocal about identifying as Muslim (Curtis, 2005). Black American Islam was indigenous to the sociopolitical factors in the Black-American community, and may have given them a

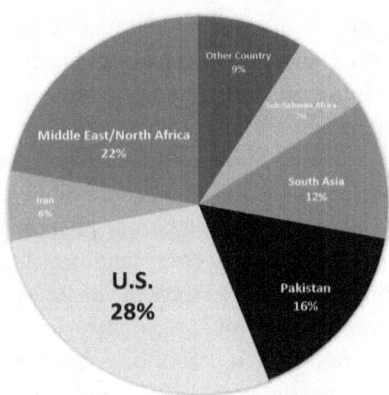

Figure 4.3. Countries of Origin.

very distinct outlook on their understanding of self, relative to the broader Muslim community. Issues of mass incarceration within inner cities like New York where their communities were thriving, were central issues in their discourse which paralleled some of the key issues of concern that Black Americans beyond Muslims experience (Dawson, 1994; McCloud, 2006). Black-American Muslims make up 20% of the Muslim-American population (Pew, 2017). The most prominent Muslim-American figures are predominantly Black Americans, from Malcolm X to Muhammad Ali, and the influence of Black Muslims on elements of the Civil Rights Movement, and particularly within art forms, like the early development of hip-hop, distinguish their contribution to both Black-American and Muslim-American communities (Abdul Khabeer, 2016).

Recently arrived Muslims from immigrant countries brought a different sociopolitical context with them. While there are traces of immigrant Muslims coming to work in the farmlands in California, and settling in New York City, the increase of Muslim immigrants did not occur until 1965 (Bakalian & Bozorgmehr, 2009). The 1965 Immigration and Naturalization Act shifted the country's immigration policy permitting a specific *kind* of immigrant to enter. Immigrants with skilled labor were encouraged to enter, and for the immigrant Muslim communities, this meant a sizeable portion of individuals from India, Pakistan, and various parts of the Middle East (Bakalian & Bozorgmehr, 2009). This brought individuals who happened to come from Muslim-majority countries, but who ranged in actual religious observance, with a sizeable portion holding a secular religious identity. This also brought sectarian distinctions, with a sizeable Shi'a population coming from Lebanon and Iran. These two sects have different political orientations that have served as points of tension in Muslim majority countries like Pakistan and Lebanon (Bakalian & Bozorgmehr, 2009). Moreover, from the 1980s forward, immigrants coming from Muslim—majority countries have been from varying socioeconomic backgrounds, with people seeking refuge from wars in Somalia, Sudan, Afghanistan, Iraq, and Syria (Bilici, 2012). Therefore, even among immigrants, the most recently arrived may have a different outlook from the 1965 wave of immigrant Muslims.

It must be noted that Muslim communal spaces are distinct by subgroups. Congregationally, the 2011 study of mosques in the United States shows that 75% of mosques are predominantly attended and run by one ethnic group—either South Asian, Black or Arab American (Bagby et al., 2011). The histories, countries, and social contexts of people that make up Muslim communities in the U.S. represent a spectrum of peoples and leave room for great variation in how they see their identities complicated by the intersection of class, race, sectarian differences, and religious observance, amongst other issues (Elliott, 2008). Given this variation, one cannot expect Muslims within diverse communities to behave or believe in monolithic terms. However, in an era of neo-racism, they are treated as a monolith—a distinct 'suspicious other.' As a result, Muslims from distinct backgrounds have sought to build commonality based on shared experiences of discrimination.

Racialization and Group Identity Theory

One of the ways to examine the consequences of neo-racism is to investigate how it affects the way diverse communities perceive the element of their identity that is racialized. In the case of Muslims, can the identity of being Muslim be one that people across subgroups attach to? How will this newly formed identity be politically consequential? The diversity and distinct social cleavages that exist for Muslims parallel what has occurred for other minority groups, namely Asian Americans and Latinos. Like Muslims, Asian Americans and Latinos form a group boundary that is inclusive of peoples from many different countries of origin and cultural backgrounds (Jones-Correa & Leal,1996; Leal, 1996: Lien, 1994; Lien et al., 2003; López & Espíritu, 1990; Padilla, 1984). There is substantive evidence to suggest they would see themselves as distinct subgroups were it not for their ascribed connection by society's dominant groups.

This lumping of a diverse body of Muslims into one entity that is seen as incompatible with the rest of society is what theories of racialization address (Bonilla-Silva, 2013; Naber & Jamal, 2008; Omi & Winant, 1986). In thinking about identity formation, it is important to emphasize that group membership is often defined from the outside. Race is a social construction that outside actors superimpose on groups of peoples (Balibar, 1991; Bonilla-Silva, 2013; Omi & Winant, 1986). Beyond institutions, the role of discourse on Muslims being "inherently violent" or having "cultural incompatibility" with the West suggests language that is not explicitly racial, but is, in fact, still racial (Balibar, 1991; Bonilla-Silva, 2013). With the external process, identity scholars turn to examining whether individuals have internalized these ascribed group identifications and if so, to what degree and to what end?

Attachment to Group Identity

Attachment to a group identity is one of the main ways that identity researchers have examined whether minorities connect to the social identities that are associated with them. Attachment to group identity has been an important factor in predicting and explaining how the adoption of such identities influence political behavior, particularly in the case of Blacks, Asian Americans, and Latinos (Huddy, 2013; Tajfel, 1981; Tajfel & Turner, 1979). Group identity taps into a psychological sense of attachment within a group. In order to explore whether this process is occurring for people who fall under the broad umbrella term of "Muslim," one must understand whether individuals who connect with their Muslim identity understand what factors influence that attachment. This is important to understand because attachment to a collective group identity often holds political meaning for other racialized groups (Lien et al., 2003; Masuoka, 2006; Sanchez, 2006).

There were, and are, very specific conditions at play that make it plausible for Muslim Americans to create a sense of a broader group identity. Not only have Muslims as a group come to be seen as one broad collective, they have also become "racialized." whereby they are grouped together and treated as a subordinate group (Cainkar, 2009; Jamal, 2008). Thus, while individuals may have viewed themselves first by another identity—like Iranian Americans—the process of racialization emphasizes their religious identity over other components that comprise their individual backgrounds. Thus, it lumps people across distinct communities together under one broader umbrella identity—in this case, being Muslim. Undoubtedly, the neo-race era, and the process of racialization influence the likelihood of disparate groups attaching to a pan-communal group identity.

Muslim Group Identity

In order to understand how Muslims in the United States felt, this analysis drew on data from the 2011 Pew Survey of American Muslims, which included a nationally representative sample of 1,033 adult Muslims residing in the United States.[1] Conducted during Obama's first term, Pew asked respondents, "Do you think of yourself first as an American or first as a Muslim?" Respondent were given response options of American, Muslim, or Both equally.[2]

Figure 4.4 presents the distribution of respondents and whether they said they identified as "Muslim," "American," or "Both." As the figure highlights, the majority of the respondents, 48%, identified primarily as Muslim. 31.5% of respondents identified primarily as American, and 20.4% identified as both Muslim and American. While there is a difference between how people from different countries of origin responded to the question, the difference was not statistically significant whereby it would be important to make distinctions.

The study revealed important findings on the relationship between group identity and socio-contextual factors.[3] Furthermore, what did turn out to be statistically significant, was the experience Muslims had with discrimination. Experiences of discrimination were found to have an influence in choosing to identify exclusively as Muslim. The distinction to consider is the difference between people who reported never having experienced discrimination compared to those who had encountered one discriminatory experience.

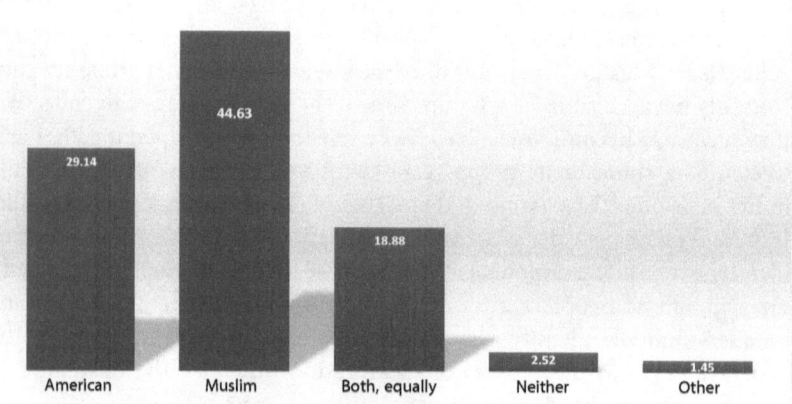

Figure 4.4. Discrimination and Identity.

It is important to note that hate crimes targeted toward Muslim Americans continued to increase. From 1997 to 1999, the Department of Justice reported 39 incidents that were targeted hate-related incidents that were anti-Muslim. That number has steadily climbed since. In 2005, 128 incidents and 146 offenses were reported, which is triple the number from the late nineties. That number has continued to steadily increase, whereby in 2006, 156 incidents and 191 offenses were reported, involving 208 victims (DOJ, 2006). By 2016, which served as the final year of Obama's presidency, 307 incidents were reported (Petulla, 2017).

With instances of discrimination serving as an important predictor of identity selection as exclusively as Muslim, the consequences of hate crimes on an individual Muslim's identity process are substantive. When subgroups of respondents are compared, the likelihood for an individual to identify exclusively as Muslim increases for individuals who have encountered a discriminatory experience, compared to those who have not. In other words, it often took one discriminatory encounter to influence members of Muslim communities to identify exclusively as Muslim. Experiences with discrimination have also been a central mechanism in predicting attachment to a racial and ethnic group identity for Latinos, Asian Americans, and Black Americans. The implications are telling, as they provide evidence of how the neo-race climate has influenced Muslims and others. Yet, given that being Muslim is not an artificial construct, but one based on inclusion within a faith-based community, it is important to be careful of the differences that a Muslim group identity has in comparison to non-faith-based minority groups.

Discussion

Looking at the history of Muslim communities, and the opinions of Muslims in the United States during the Obama administration is telling. The neo-racism era has, as the results suggested, played a role in influencing how Muslims view their identity. Specifically, encountering discrimination is associated with connecting more closely with one's religious identity. The findings suggested that the sociopolitical climate has played an important rule influencing the way a diverse body of peoples now attach to a broader group identity. During the Obama era, the survey results suggested that there is an association between Muslims attaching to a Muslim identity and their encounters with discrimination. Those who have experienced discrimination are more likely to identify exclusively as Muslim, compared to respondents who have not encountered a discriminatory experience.

Their cultural distinctions have been sublimated in an effort to thrive under the pressure of an ascribed identity.

Conclusion

So, who gets to say Hussein? This chapter highlighted the sociopolitical climate during President Obama's presidential campaigns and during his tenure in office. The manifestations of neo-racism were evident from explicit government policies targeting Muslims to the subtle ways it affected people thought to be Muslim—such as Barack Hussein Obama. The sensitivity around his middle name was and is indicative of the climate surrounding Muslims in the U.S. It may have pushed President Obama to be more cautious in some of his public engagement with Muslims during his time in office given the birther movement's attempts to use his connection to Muslims as a smear tactic against him. These dynamics spotlight the explicit and subtle ways in which neo-racism affected Muslims and those perceived to be Muslim, especially during Obama's two terms.

The relationship between a Muslim's experience with discrimination and her/his connection to a group identity is an important consideration. The social context for Muslim Americans has shifted. Muslim racialization and the potential influence this has on attachment to group identity is powerful, and the process is evident based on the survey results presented. With President Obama's tenure in office complete, the rise of the Trump Administration suggests that this process will only continue, and life for Muslims is likely to become more complicated for Muslims in the United States. President Trump has already done away with public gestures that court Muslims such as the White House iftar dinner. Even more explicit has been the 2017 travel ban that President Trump announced, executive order 13769, titled "Protecting the Nation from Foreign Terrorist Entry into the United States" (Liptak, 2017). This order, more commonly known in public discourse as the "Muslim ban," barred travel from seven Muslim-majority countries (Carasik, 2017). While the U.S. Supreme Court has limited the full implementation of the order, it will be important to assess how the more explicit targeting of Muslims impacts their group identity formation in this changing political landscape under President Trump. If the evidence from President Obama's time in office is any indication, the Trump era may influence Muslims, from diverse backgrounds and segregated communities, to continue to build shared experiences that may serve as important grounds for community mobilization in the face of continued rising anti-Muslim sentiment.

References

Abdul Khabeer, S. (2016). *Muslim Cool: Race Religion and Hip Hop in the United States*. New York: NYU Press.

Ali, W., Duss, M., Fang, L., Keyes, S., & Shakir, F. (2011). *Fear, Inc. The Roots of the Islamophobia Network in America*. Washington, DC: Center for American Progress.

Alsultany, E. (2012). *Arabs and Muslims in the Media : Race and Representation After 9/11*. New York: NYU Press.

Alsultany, E. (2016). Arabs and Muslims in the U.S.—American Media Before and After 9/11, in *Media and Minorities: Questions of Representation from an International Perspective*, Georg Ruhrmann, Peter Widmann, and Yasemin Shoman, Eds., Göttigen, Germany: Vandenhoech & Ruprecht, 104–117.

American National Election Studies. (2008). Time Series Study. Ann Arbor, MI: University of Michigan, Center for Political Studies.

American National Election Studies. (2012). Time Series Study. Ann Arbor, MI: University of Michigan, Center for Political Studies.

Asian American Legal Defense and Education Fund. (2013). Mapping Muslims: NYPD Spying and its Impact on American Muslims. Policy Paper: AALDEF.

Bail, C. A. (2012). The fringe effect: Civil society organizations and the evolution of media discourse about Islam since the September 11th attacks. *American Sociological Review*, 77(6), 855–879.

Balibar, E., & Wallerstein, I. M. (1991). *Race, Nation, Class: Ambiguous Identities*. London: Verso.

BBC News. (2015). History of calling Barack Obama a Muslim." Available at http://www.bbc.com/news/av/world-us-canada-34293947/a-history-of-calling-barack-obama-a-muslim

Beydoun, K. A. (2016, February 4). Un-mosquing Obama's first US mosque visit. *Al Jazeera*, 1–4.

Bonilla-Silva, E. (2013). *Racism without Racists: Color-Blind Racism and the Persistence of Racial Inequality in America*. New York: Rowman and Littlefield.

Cainkar, L. (2009). *Homeland Insecurity: The Arab and Muslim American Experience After 9/11*. New York: Russell Sage Foundation.

Curtis, E. (2013). "The Study of American Muslims: a History." In J. Hammer & O. Safi. *The Cambridge Companion to American Islam*. New York: Cambridge University Press.

Elliot. (2007, March 11). "Between Black and Immigrant Muslims, an Uneasy Alliance." *New York Times*, 1–15. Retrieved from http://www.nytimes.com/2007/03/11/nyregion/11muslim.html

Elliott, A. (2010, April 18). White House Quietly Courts Muslims in U.S. *New York Times*. Retrieved from http://www.nytimes.com/2010/04/19/us/politics/19muslim.html

Esposito, J. L., & Kalın, Ibrahim. (2011). *Islamophobia: The Challenge of Pluralism in the 21st Century*. Oxford: Oxford University Press.

Goldman, A., & Apuzzo, M. (2012). "With cameras, informants, NYPD eyed mosques." *The Associated Press*. Retrieved from https://www.ap.org/ap-in-the-news/2012/with-cameras-informants-nypd-eyed-mosques

Gurin P, Miller, A. H., & Gurin, G. (1980). Stratum identification and consciousness. *Soc. Psychol. Q.* 43, 30–47.

Jamal, A. (2005). The Political Participation and Engagement of Muslim Americans: Mosque Involvement and Group Consciousness, *American Politics Research*, 33(4), 521–544.

Jamal, A. (2008). Civil Liberties and the Otherization of Arab and Muslim Americans. In J. A. Editor & N. N. Editor (Eds.), *Race and Arab Americans Before and After 9/11* (114–130). Syracuse, NY: Syracuse University Press.

Jamal, A. (2013). Demographics, political participation, and representation. In O. Safi & J. Hamer (Eds.), *The Cambridge Companion on American Islam*. Oxford: Oxford University Press.

Jamal, A., & Naber, N. (2005). *Race and Arab Americans Before and After 9/11: From Invisible Citizens to Visible Subjects*. Syracuse, NY: Syracuse University Press.

Johnson, J., & Hauslohner, A. May 20, 2017. 'I think Islam hates us': A timeline of Trump's comments about Islam and Muslims." *The Washington Post*. Available at: https://www.washingtonpost.com/news/post-politics/wp/2017/05/20/i-think-islam-hates-us-a-timeline-of-trumps-comments-about-islam-and-muslims/?utm_term=.6b1474c64014

Jones-Correa, M., & Leal, D. (1996). Becoming 'Hispanic': Secondary Panethnic Identification Among Latin American-Origin Populations in the United States. *Hispanic Journal of Behavioral Sciences*, 18, 214–54.

Junn J., & Masuoka, N. (2008). Asian American Identity: Shared Racial Status and Political Context. *Perspectives on Politics*, 6(4), 729–740.

Lee, T. (2008). From Shared Demographic Categories to Common Political Destinies? Immigration and the Link from Racial Identity to Group Politics. *DuBois Review*, 4, 433–456.

Lien P-T. (2001). Voting participation: race, gender, and the comparative status of Asian American women. See Chang 2001, 173–193.

Lien, P., Conway, M. M., & Wong, J. (2003)."The Contours and Sources of Ethnic Identity Choices Among Asian Americans. *Social Science Quarterly*, 84(2), 461–481.

Liptak, A. (2017). "Supreme Court Allows Trump Travel Ban to Take Effect." *NYTimes*. Retrieved from: https://www.nytimes.com/2017/12/04/us/politics/trump-travel-ban-supreme-court.html

López, D., & Espíritu, Y. (1990). Panethnicity in the United States: a theoretical framework. *Ethnic and Racial Studies*, 13, 198–224.

Lyall, S. (2010). In Shift, U.S. Lifts Visa Curbs on Professor. *NYTimes*. Retrieved from: http://www.nytimes.com/2010/01/21/world/europe/21london.html

Martin, J., & Parnes, A. (2008)."McCain: Obama not an Arab, crowd boos. *Politico*. Available at https://www.politico.com/story/2008/10/mccain-obama-not-an-arab-crowd-boos-014479

Masuoka, N. (2006). Together They Become One: Examining the Predictors of Panethnic Group Consciousness Among Asian Americans and Latinos. *Social Science Quarterly,* 87, 5, & 993–1011.

McClain, P. D., Carew, J. J., Walton, E, Jr., & Watts, C. S. (2009). Group Membership, Group Identity and Group Consciousness: Evolving Racial Identity in American Politics. *Annual Review of Political Science,* 12, 471–485.

"Muslim Americans: No Signs of Growth in Alienation or Support for Extremism." Pew Research Center, Washington, DC (2011). http://www.people-press.org/2011/08/30/muslim-americans-no-signs-of-growth-in-alienation-or-support-for-extremism/

Miller, A. H., Gurin, P., Gurin, G., & Malanchuk, O. (1981). Group Consciousness and Political Participation. *American Journal of Political Science,* 25(3), 494–511.

Nobles, M. (2000). *Shades of Citizenship: Race and the Census in Modern Politics.* Stanford, CA: Stanford University Press.

Omi, M., & Winant, H. (1986). *Racial Formation in the United States: From the 1960s to the 1980s.* London and New York: Routledge.

Padilla, F. (1985). *Latino Ethnic Consciousness: The Case of Mexican Americans and Puerto Ricans in Chicago.* Notre Dame, IN: University of Notre Dame Press.

Petulla, S. (2017). The number of hate crimes rose in 2016. CNN. Retrieved from https://www.cnn.com/2017/11/13/politics/hate-crimes-fbi-2016-rise/index.html

Powell, C. (2008). Interview by T. Brokaw. *Meet the Press.* [Television broadcast]. Washington DC: NBC News.

Read, J. (2005). "Discrimination and Identity Formation in a Post-9/11 Era." In J. A. Editor & N. N. Editor (Eds.), *Race and Arab Americans Before and After 9/11.* Syracuse, NY: Syracuse University Press.

Reevell, J. (2015). A history of calling Barack Obama a Muslim. Retrieved from http://www.bbc.com/news/av/world-us-canada-34293947/a-history-of-calling-barack-obama-a-muslim

Sanchez, G. R. (2006). The Role of Group Consciousness in Political Participation Among Latinos in the United States. *American Politics Research,* 34(4), 427–450.

Sanchez, G. R. (2008). Latino Group Consciousness and Perceptions of Commonality with African Americans. *Social Science Quarterly,* 89(2), 428–444.

Serwer, A. (2013, April 4). Whatever Happened to the Obama Administration's Review of NYPD Spying? *Mother Jones,* pp. 1–6. Retrieved from https://www.motherjones.com/politics/2013/04/nypd-muslim-surveillance-justice-department-eric-holder/

Shaheen, J. G. (2015). *Reel bad Arabs: How Hollywood vilifies a people.* Northampton, MA: Olive Branch Press.

Waddell, K. (2016). America Already Had a Muslim Registry. *The Atlantic.* Available at: https://www.theatlantic.com/technology/archive/2016/12/america-already-had-a-muslim-registry/511214

Winant, H. (2004). *The New Politics of Race.* Minneapolis MN: The University of Minnesota Press.
Wong, J. S., Lien P. T., & Conway, M. M. (2005). Group-based resources and political participation among Asian Americans. *American Politics Research,* 33, 545–576.

5

The End of AIDS?

A Critical Analysis of the National HIV/AIDS Strategy

Andrew R. Spieldenner, Tomeka M. Robinson, Anjuliet Woodruffe

"Getting to Zero" was the theme of World AIDS Day 2011, with heightened emphasis placed on the need to advance education, treatment, and prevention in regard to the HIV/AIDS epidemic in the United States and around the world (White House, 2011). Since his inauguration, President Barack Obama annually made a patriotic appeal to the humanity and charitable nature of the American people to continue to fight the disease, which in its early years was one of the "most devastating pandemics." The goal of Obama's efforts was to create an "AIDS-free generation." Stressing his appreciation for the heroes who courageously shared their stories, Obama attempted to motivate Americans to persist in fighting to create a world where every person living with HIV (PLHIV)[1] could have access to affordable care and treatment. However, the quest for new treatments that can reduce infection rates does not eliminate the need for educating the public, particularly higher risk groups, about disease prevention. HIV still carries a powerful stigma and advances in treatment can potentially increase reckless behaviors.

The White House Office of National AIDS Policy (ONAP) produced the National HIV/AIDS Strategy (NHAS) in 2010 (ONAP, 2010). This plan was the culmination of fourteen town halls conducted across the country, with input from key public health leaders and researchers. President Barack Obama was the first U.S. president to produce a national strategy—and the United States is the last of the G8 countries to have one. Ironically, this is far after the U.S. had been requiring other countries receiving U.S. President's Emergency Plan for AIDS Relief (PEPFAR) funds to have a national strategy to deal with HIV. Soon after the NHAS, President Obama and Secretary of State Hillary Clinton proclaimed the "End of AIDS" in talks at the International AIDS Conference 2012 and other public events (Maulsby et al., 2016). This practice continued, as various state governors and activists utilized the "End of AIDS" as a mantra to organize government support for the issue (Cuomo, 2013). However, the rhetoric within these "End of AIDS" initiatives and the National HIV/AIDS Strategy have constructions around race—and particularly Blackness—that would limit its possibility.

An Intersectional and Race-Based Critique of Public Policy

We want to look at the National HIV/AIDS Strategy within the broader frameworks of intersectionality and Critical Race Theory. This analysis will utilize the concepts of neo-race and intersectionality in its critique of the National HIV/AIDS Strategy. We utilize intersectionality in order to better understand the dimensions of oppression and marginalization undergirding the policy. We use CRT to make explicit circuits of power and powerlessness through the processes of naming. We are rooted in self-reflexivity, and as such we position ourselves as: a cis-gendered gay multiracial Asian man living with HIV; a cis-gendered mixed-race heterosexual HIV-negative woman; and a cis-gendered heterosexual Caribbean HIV-negative woman.

Founded in Black Feminism, intersectionality demands that people account for various facets of their identity in concrete, material, and positional ways (Crenshaw, 1991). Intersectionality has encouraged the identity concatenation of race, class, gender, and sexuality in order to make explicit ways that people have access (or not) to power and opportunity, as well as how this access informs perceptions and beliefs. While this has obvious implications for socially marginalized identities—such as being gay amidst homophobia or heterosexism, being a person of color within racism, or being a woman amongst sexism, intersectionality also acknowledges the ways that discrimination can be compounded, or made invisible due to single-issue foci. In addition, intersectionality is flexible, and can be used to explore norms and power in relation to a wide range of identities, including health condition, immigration status, age, religious beliefs, and experience with activities considered illicit in society (such as sex work or substance use).

Critical race theory (CRT) provides a way to look at how power is enacted through discussions of race. Delgado and Stefancic (2012) provide productive ways to utilize CRT in examining legal or policy documents: rigorous analysis of neoliberalism at work; structural determinism in legal thought; and intersectionality. Neoliberalism is a discourse that involves capitalist markets in understanding and solving social issues such as public health, education, deregulation, and free trade. As such, neoliberal models are often conservative in their approach to social justice or health disparities. CRT provides a framework to unpack the cultural notions that undergird the policy or legislative acts, especially as these assumptions approach identity and race.

Race was a central frame in the Obama Presidency, marking most of the administration's endeavors and criticisms. As the first African-American—or even non-White—President, his actions and rhetoric were consistently racialized. Even his birth was questioned in the aggressive "birther" campaign whose membership demanded a paper birth certificate to prove his American birth. Obama and his administration were imbricated within race overtly and covertly, as he became both "all-American" as the President, and a potential foreign threat in the birther discourse (Pham, 2015). We see the obvious need to incorporate CRT in the examination of any of Obama's policies (or their reception).

This analysis looks specifically at public policy as a discourse. We see the National HIV/AIDS Strategy as a marker of the government's role in HIV and the ways that people living with HIV and Black people are constructed in this vision. We also see the National HIV/AIDS Strategy as a tool that organizations and people use to make sense of the epidemic.

Public policy is an important sign of discourse. It sheds light on the social conventions, and is clear evidence of the values promoted by a government or legislator. Woodside-Jiron (2004) remarked "policies define how we are to act and by what rules we must abide" (p. 174). Public policy presents social rules that, generally, come with consequences for violating them. In the early 1980s, any public discussion of HIV/AIDS was considered taboo and public policy regarding testing and treatment maintained a discourse of identity shaming and blaming (Adam, 1989).

Defining the National HIV/AIDS Strategy

The goals of the NHAS are straightforward: reduce HIV infection rates, increase the number of people living with HIV with access to medical services, and decrease HIV-related health disparities (ONAP, 2010; ONAP, 2015a). To reduce HIV infection rates, the NHAS proposes to increase HIV testing and a targeted approach to HIV prevention in communities where HIV seroprevalence is highest.[2] To increase access to health services, the NHAS proposes to increase access to Anti-Retroviral medications (ARVs) for people living with HIV, as well as to address first-time linkage to medical appointments and housing for people living with HIV. To reduce HIV-related health disparities, the NHAS proposes to focus on African Americans, particularly African-American gay and bisexual men—who bear a disproportionate burden in the HIV epidemic domestically. These goals and strategies are admirable, but remain embedded in a neoliberal ideology about HIV.

In 2015, the NHAS was revised with a timeline until 2020 (ONAP, 2015a; ONAP, 2015b). Several key changes occurred in the language of the NHAS: the identification of several more identities; the inclusion of HIV stigma; and the highlighting of interventions such as HIV Pre-Exposure Prophylaxis (PrEP) and virologic suppression. These changes were lauded by several community-based organizations and policy groups, demonstrating, for them, advances in both discourse and scientific knowledge.

The NHAS has a large impact in domestic HIV efforts, involving several government agencies. Each agency must identify goals and objectives that fall in line with the overall NHAS. Some involve only nominal resources, such as adding HIV testing in ICE facilities. Other agencies have extensive resources involved, such as the entirety of the 2015 United States Centers for Disease Control and Prevention (CDC) approximate $788 million HIV prevention portfolio for fiscal year 2017 (CDC, 2016d). The NHAS has informed initiatives like the CDC High Impact Prevention (HIP), where the CDC has directed its funding toward community-level and population-level prevention efforts in high HIV-incidence regions (CDC, 2015b). This turned resources away from individual-level intervention work, as well as low HIV-incidence states.

For this analysis, we will look at how racial identity is deployed in the NHAS. In particular, we want to look at the ways that Black gay and bisexual men and Black women are discursively constructed in the NHAS, and how issues of HIV are framed by race in it.

Gender and Sexuality: Bounded by Blackness?

In the United States, identity categories usually pivot on a single difference (gender, sexuality, or race), and where race is not named, it is assumed to be White. In the NHAS, two identities—women and men who have sex with men (MSM)—are identified as Black throughout the NHAS.

This race-ing of identities presents different visions of the identities, with perhaps unintended consequences.

The NHAS invokes Black women as the sole identifier in "women," with perhaps unintended consequences. In the United States, Black women represent the largest part of the HIV epidemic amongst women, including new diagnoses, current women living with HIV, and the highest mortality rate. Naming this category explicitly Black centers Black women in an unprecedented way in a government document on HIV. It purports to advance the needs of Black women within the context of HIV services and advocacy.

Of course, this implies that organizations, policymakers, and people have the same understanding of what the term Black women entails. Using intersectionality, we can see that the term "Black women" can be used to discuss a wide range of women including, amongst others, heterosexual church-going, middle-class Black women, Black women who are sex workers, Black women with a history of engagement with law enforcement, Black disabled women, and Black bisexual women and lesbians. The nuance about the population gets lost in the NHAS. Within CRT, we can see how the term "Black women" is used to represent a broad symbol of people, with little specificity in the unpacking of the category. This has material impact on those Black women who may be more marginalized due to substance use, socioeconomic class, sexuality, immigration, and/or disability.

Similar work is done in the MSM category. MSM is a broad term emerging in public health as a way to describe a behavior, rather than a community. It is meant to include gay, bisexual, trans, and other men who have sex with men—some of whom may not identify as "gay" or part of the gay community. Its use in public health has been somewhat double-edged—oftentimes erasing the gay and bisexual identities it is meant to include. The use of "MSM" in the everyday language of community-based organizations and their HIV programs—rather than "gay" or "bisexual"—also helps to obfuscate the discomfort people and organizations may have with gay and bisexual identities and cultures. Further, there has been considerable critique of a gay identity that does not include an intersectional approach. This non-raced gay male figure leads to a series of thoughts such as, amongst others: all gay men are White; gayness is somehow a product of White culture and can be therefore denied within communities of color; and gay men of color are aberrations and therefore do not exist within communities of color or its institutions.

For Black gay, bisexual, trans, and other men who have sex with men, the category of MSM has long had Black-focused initiatives within HIV public health work. Within the context of the NHAS, the racializing of MSM with "Black" does not further explicate what would make Black MSM differ from other (especially White) MSM for service providers, policymakers, and clinicians who may not be trained in the nuances of Black queer healthcare. The community contexts about risk, survival, and healthcare access are not discussed or even referred to other resources. It would be possible to read the NHAS and assume that Black queer men have little differences with their White counterparts, and that sexuality is their primary organizing principle within HIV—not other issues which may be relevant in the particular constellations of identity such as sex work, substance use, mental health, socioeconomics, engagement with policing, immigration, disability, age and/or even sexual positioning.

The NHAS explicitly connects both female and gay identity with a Black racial marker in the HIV epidemic. While this naming of race, gender, and sexuality is important in the realm of representation and visibility, we question the position of these identities as objects of health care services and policy. For one, it limits the ways that other communities of color are made visible within HIV. For another, these categories serve to flatten any nuanced understanding of what these communities do. Using a CRT lens, we see that representation is not enough, that the inclusion of race marks other unspoken concerns. In what ways does the explicitness of Black women and Black MSM trouble the waters for institutions and communities less familiar with this specificity?

Defining Vulnerability through Race

Health policy is not just about a practice: it illustrates a number of social discourses related to the issue (Woodside-Jiron, 2004). The NHAS has the potential to contribute to problematic discourse about Black women, Black MSM, and HIV. We use CRT to examine how power is exerted on these Black identities within the NHAS. With these groups as the only named groups (in terms of race and gender, or race and sexuality), this could have the unintended effect of naturalizing HIV diagnoses for these populations. When we talk about naturalizing HIV diagnoses, we do not mean that the health policy produces HIV within the population in any particular way, rather we are talking to the perception that these groups are *supposed* to contract HIV in this construction. That particular narrative is problematic within the community and can impact HIV service provision.

The lack of nuanced and intentional centering of Black experiences in the articulation of the NHAS has other consequences. Often, public health information is released without acknowledging the potential impact.

As an exemplar, the CDC announced that Black gay and bisexual men had a 50% likelihood of being exposed to HIV in their lifetimes (CDC, 2016b). This information was released without acknowledging that Black gay and bisexual men are already marked by HIV, stigmatized within the community as carriers of HIV (Bird & Voisin, 2013), and targeted by health departments and pharmaceutical companies with HIV-specific messages in public (Spieldenner & Castro, 2010). The impact of the CDC statistic is problematic, as it situates HIV risk and exposure as exclusive and definitive to Black gay and bisexual men, rather than as an outcome of a mathematical probability model. Amongst Black gay and bisexual men, the community could see HIV-diagnosis as inevitable. Outside of the community, service providers and other communities—including White LGBT community members—could see this as typical. Within this narrative, the only surprising (and within the framework of "innocence," the only worthwhile) HIV-diagnosis would be again amongst the White gay community. Therefore, if a Black gay, bisexual, trans, or man who has sex with a man contracts HIV, it is expected. Shock and public outcry occurs in this context when the White gay community continues to acquire HIV.

Naturalizing HIV-diagnoses can encourage HIV-related stigma within the community. In this particular case, the presumption of HIV could cause community members to treat all Black gay, bisexual, trans, and other men who have sex with men as if they already have the disease and treat them accordingly. HIV-related stigma devalues people in specific ways: "dirty" or tainted via infection, morally corrupt through sex or substance use, and/or irresponsible and therefore deserving of the disease. People living with HIV may experience stigma from friends and family, and refuse to commit to medication or clinical visits due to fear of losing their support network. Poor health outcomes from HIV are more likely if people living with HIV do not consistently stay in clinical care. Using an intersectional lens, clinical care becomes further compounded for Black, queer men with the presence of HIV, queer sexuality, and Blackness—all stigmatized conditions.

Black gay and bisexual men and Black women already tend to face significant societal discrimination and HIV-related stigma amplifies feelings of intolerance and exploitation, even among health care practitioners (CDC, 2016b; CDC, 2016c). These get enacted throughout the healthcare process where there is a general mistrust of health experts to communicate the truth about HIV (Herek et al., 2002) or treat PLHIV with respect and not disdain. Clinicians and clinic staff may believe that people living with HIV acquired the disease through immoral or irresponsible actions, and therefore treat them accordingly (doubting information, nonverbal communication cues of disgust or disrespect, not keeping confidentiality by speaking the person's name or condition loudly, etc.). Even with equal access to health care, differences in viral suppression persist among people living with HIV across racial lines (Castel et al., 2016). These differences are perhaps due to a healthcare system that is set up for a White, professional, health literate, empowered user, rather than the majority of Black women, and Black gay and bisexual men.

At the institutional level, this discourse furthers the notion that White individuals do not get HIV. The myth of White supremacy and superiority becomes perpetuated by this framing, a myth that also serves to deny the existence of White people living with HIV. Therefore, in discussions at the service and institutional level, White people living with HIV are not visible or acknowledged in the pursuit of obtaining the "consumer" voice (when that consumer is defined as Black and female, or Black and gay). The position of White people living with HIV is undermined within a context that pretends they do not exist, their challenges with HIV care are irrelevant, or that they do not deserve a voice. We contend that, while White people living with HIV tend to have more access to advocacy or policy tables, the silencing of their voice completely within an HIV framework does not advance a useful public health framework. Rather we would center Black women and Black gay and bisexual men, which would insist on inclusive (rather than exclusive) frameworks for participation at a meaningful level.

Problematizing Populations Rather than Institutions

The NHAS does not address institutional barriers; instead it looks at populations as willing participants in health care and much of the language is about Black MSM and Black women being more involved in HIV testing and treatment without addressing issues at the institutional levels. We assert that one lesson from CRT is that power is institutionalized, and that people do not have the same scope of powers that institutions do. In this way, health care is not a neutral phenomenon: rather, it constructs and disciplines its subjects in the health care process in a variety of ways.

In the seminal text *Boundaries of Blackness*, Cohen (1999) identified the ways that the traditional African-American organizing institutions, the church and the Black press, were passive at the start of the HIV epidemic, if not overtly antagonistic. HIV has largely been associated with substance use, sex, and homosexuality—all behaviors that defy the respectability politics that have characterized much of the African-American church and the Black press. The Black church in the United States is more than just a religious institution—it provides a moral function that helps to shape collective identity and form community. When the Black church promotes homophobia and deters sexual freedom, religious leaders need to address homosexuality and other forms of sexual freedom to focus on HIV testing experiences and HIV education (Ojikutu et al., 2014). HIV's connection to substance use, sex, and homosexuality has ensured that the disease would be heavily stigmatized. Goffman (1963) defines stigma as "an attribute that links a person to an undesirable stereotype, leading other people to reduce the bearer from a whole and usual person to a tainted, discounted one" (p. 11). Discussions of HIV often unveil public anxieties that are attributed to gender identity, sexuality, ethnicity, and race. In fact, according to Herek et al. (2002), "[PLHIV] . . . have been shunned by strangers and family members, discriminated against in employment and healthcare, driven from their homes, and subjected to physical abuse" (p. 371). Traditional African-American institutions need to work through their limitations and historical trouble dealing with HIV, Black women, and Black MSM. The religiosity aspect of these institutions is neither acknowledged nor dealt with in the NHAS vision, and this religiosity permeates so deeply that even the most casual institutional member feels it.

Traditional African-American institutions are not the only spaces that have struggled with HIV, Black women, and Black MSM: traditional public health organizations have faced similar challenges. HIV health disparities persist for Black women, including lower retention in care, lower rates of ART prescriptions, and lower viral suppression rates than their White counterparts. These disparities indicate that Black women are more likely to have health complications due to HIV. This is further exacerbated by structural racism in the United States where African Americans are more likely to live in poverty, be uninsured, and have lower quality health services available. In the U.S., Black women are more likely than any other demographic of women to have HIV. According to the CDC, Black women constituted 62% of all women diagnosed with HIV in 2014 (CDC, 2015, p. 29). In terms of lifetime risk, 1 in 48 Black women in the United States will likely be diagnosed with HIV, compared to 1 in 227 Hispanic women and 1 in 880 White women (CDC, 2016c). As with other PLHIV, Black women living with HIV have to deal with stigma, even in the healthcare system.

Additionally, thirty years into the HIV epidemic, Black gay and bisexual men are disproportionately impacted by the disease in terms of infection rates and mortality from the disease. Whereas Black gay and bisexual men accounted for less than 10% of the overall U.S. population, in 2014, Black gay, bisexual, and other MSM constituted over one-quarter of all new HIV diagnoses in the country. In terms of overall risk of HIV infection during a lifetime, Black gay and bisexual men have the highest probability of being exposed to HIV of any group or demographic in the U.S., with numbers as high as 50% (CDC, 2016b).

The impact of HIV cannot be explained by a lack of HIV prevention services since Black gay and bisexual men have been in the forefront of HIV prevention initiatives in the United States. CRT can however, examine how White privilege manifests in regard to homonormativity, wealth disparity, healthcare access, and education among this risk group. Indeed, as Coston and Kimmel (2012) state, "[w]hen one is privileged by class, or race or gender or sexuality, one rarely sees exactly how the dynamics of privilege work" (p. 97). The CDC acknowledges "socioeconomic issues associated with poverty—including limited access to high-quality health care, housing, and HIV prevention education . . . may explain why African Americans have worse outcomes on the HIV continuum of care, including lower rates of linkage to care, retention in care, being prescribed HIV treatment [Anti-Retroviral Therapy], and viral suppression" (CDC, 2016a, para. 8). Even in this framing, the CDC proffers a situation where those most impacted—African Americans, in this case—are the focus ("African Americans have worse outcomes") without addressing those processes most likely to provide the solutions ("linkage to care, retention in care, being prescribed HIV treatment"). The failure on the part of service providers and institutions remains unnamed. This silence is furthered in the NHAS.

While these factors for HIV vulnerability are recognized by CDC, the NHAS Implementation Plan does little to address them. In the 2015 update, the NHAS Implementation Plan asks to "explore opportunities to focus on HIV-related disparities" in only one agency (ONAP, 2015b, p. 23). In the rest, Black gay and bisexual men are relegated as service recipients of the agencies who have provided HIV risk reduction, substance use and other HIV services to Black gay and bisexual men for over two decades (CDC, 2007). It is unclear how significant reduction in HIV acquisition, reduced HIV mortality, and improved health outcomes will occur without new strategies.

The 2015 NHAS update identifies Black women as a priority. Black women are included in the 2015 NHAS in similar ways as Black gay and bisexual men and, in fact, in the same sections (ONAP, 2015b). Rather than unpacking or re-centering the implementation plans on the needs of Black women, agencies are required to provide the same services as before. The one exception is the vague remand of "explore opportunities to focus on HIV-related disparities" in one agency (ONAP, 2015b, p. 23).

By using CRT, we see the limits of representation in the NHAS. While the policy may be to prioritize Black women and Black MSM in

HIV, the organizations providing service—whether community-based or governmental—have a far distance to go to meet the need, if history is any measure. If this distance is not considered in the timelines or resourcing, then how successful can the NHAS be? We acknowledge that the inclusion and prioritization of Black women and Black MSM are important, as discussions of race and gender, and race and sexuality, are rare; yet we question the ways that the rhetoric of intersectional approaches is invoked without concomitant resources.

The efficacy of medical treatment may lead some to presume that HIV is a purely biomedical condition, yet HIV affects other parts of a person's life. HIV can impact a person's social support, mental health, and interpersonal relationships with family and intimate partners, and socioeconomics (including cost of medical care and access to employment). These other factors remain a critical part of effectively providing the tools to "end AIDS," yet these are not as developed in the NHAS as other standard public health tools, like surveillance. An intersectional view of HIV would bring these facets into the fore.

The NHAS involves PLHIV in multiple ways, including identifying mechanisms for linking to medical care, retention in medical care, access to ART, and stigma. Leadership development was mentioned in the Strategy, but not in the Federal Action Plan. In the Federal Action Plan, people living with HIV—including Black women and Black gay and bisexual men—are relegated to very specific roles: as patients in need of clinical care, as problems in treatment adherence or medical care retention, or as victims in need of protections. These roles perpetuate a helplessness to the power deployed by institutions on people of color and other marginalized persons. People living with HIV have limited recourse outside of these domains: the increased leadership goal only asks for more opportunities from the CDC in community planning, peer educators at minority-serving colleges, and an Advisory Board at the Veterans Affairs. Finally, the protections proffered in the NHAS Federal Action Plan do not include a call to eliminate HIV criminalization laws nationally—laws which make a criminal offense the lack of disclosure, or possible exposure to bodily fluids of people living with HIV.

The NHAS frames HIV as a process of individual choices rather than an epidemic that forces structural change to ameliorate. Individual choices, in this case, include the choice of HIV prevention, the choice of an HIV test, the choice of medical care, the choice of taking treatment, and the choice of HIV disclosure. We point out that many of these are not individual choices, but exist within a larger context. For instance, the choice of HIV medical care does not take into account personal insurance, history with healthcare providers, options for culturally competent quality healthcare locally, and current stability to be in care. The structural analysis within the NHAS is lacking, and will do little to change the situation for Black gay, bisexual, trans, and other men who have sex with men, or Black women.

Conclusion

The NHAS falls short of tackling the concerns of HIV, Black gay and bisexual men, and Black women. Often, each community or issue is defined in ways that remain unaddressed in the Implementation Plan. Stigma, for instance, is a structural issue as well as a social concern yet there are only vague recommendations or requirements without practical steps (e.g., "ensure clinics are stigma-free"). Compare this vagueness with the clear instruction about immigrants: "assess the feasibility of incorporating HIV education and opt-out testing and linkage to care into the current health screening process of all undocumented immigrants in [Immigration and Customs Enforcement Health Service Corps] facilities" (ONAP, 2015b, p. 12). These discrepancies reveal several ideologies undergirding the NHAS: trickle down public health policies; and refusing to acknowledge the centrality of race in the experience of HIV.

We use the term "trickle-down public health" policies to reflect the failed economic policy of the 1980s, where profit incentives for the wealthy were meant to eventually reach the middle class and poor Americans. When this did not occur, the wealth divide between those with wealth and those without was widened exponentially. In similar ways, public health policies meant to serve a "general public" are often meant as a trickle-down approach to public health. In the meantime, issues that are central to marginalized groups are overlooked. Trickle-down public health presumes that there are acceptable losses to the long-term population health. While at an individual level, this may be true, this analysis problematizes the idea when the acceptable loss includes whole groups of peoples, whole communities whose issues are too complicated, too difficult, or too stigmatized to address.

The NHAS Implementation Plan does an inadequate job of deploying identity in productive ways. This capacity to "not name" an identity becomes problematic as silences mount. Whereas terms like "general population" or "all people" would seem to be an inclusive humanistic view, it reveals a startling exclusion—as if "not naming" an already marginalized identity is a means of repressing its visibility. Calafell (2015) writes against this urge, claiming, "many important issues regarding diversity, racism, and White supremacy must be glossed over in favor of the common good—which happens to be the good of the White hegemonic order . . . laws that protect marginalized people are ignored" (p. 27). As a public health policy, the NHAS should act against the hegemonic silence about the concerns of Black gay and bisexual men, Black women, people living with HIV, and other marginalized groups like trans individuals, immigrants, and sex workers.

The NHAS fails to acknowledge that some bodies are already marked in public health by identity. As Holloway (2011) states, "[i]n the history of medicine, populations marked as 'vulnerable' are patients whose medical care has been attached to identity" (p. 111). This identity must be central to the public health approach, especially in a health condition as stigmatized as HIV. Rather than relying on various agencies to determine how they approach identity, the NHAS might serve more productively by requiring this approach. For instance, health departments and the CDC have had particular focuses on African Americans for over a decade without centering specifically on the particular (and different) concerns of Black gay and bisexual men, and Black women (CDC, 2007). These initiatives will have limited impact as long as those most impacted are not central to public health policy, planning, and implementation.

The National HIV Strategy is rooted in a simple vision which Obama shared on World AIDS Day, that "every American could get access to life-extending care regardless of age, race, gender, ethnicity, sexual orientation, gender identity or socio-economic status" (White House, 2011, p. 2). One of the goals of the Affordable Care Act (ACA) is to ensure that Americans can have access to affordable health insurance as well as free HIV testing and, more significantly, beginning in 2014, no American would be denied health insurance coverage because of preexisting conditions and their HIV status. President Obama would have been remiss if he could not openly discuss the impact of HIV among those most impacted, including Black gay and bisexual men, Black women, and people living with HIV. From his World AIDS Day in 2011 speech, Obama said, "When new infections among young, Black gay men increase by nearly 50 percent in 3 years, we need to do more than show them that their lives matter . . . when Black women feel forgotten, even though they account for most of the new cases among women, we've got to do more" (White House, 2011). Citing that infection rates are declining worldwide but not in the United States, President Obama urged the public to consider how individuals as well as families are affected by HIV.

With this background, the NHAS has emerged as a policy tool meant to "end the AIDS epidemic," at least domestically. Yet the NHAS will never accomplish this act, as it discursively fails to address the context of HIV. For disenfranchised groups, health care and treatment discussions have adopted a neoliberal lens and a neo-race rhetoric, thus limiting the potential action possible. The health care system becomes the agency of understanding identity, health, and sexual behaviors. While President Obama continued his rhetoric of change and identified Black gay and bisexual men and Black women in his discussion of HIV, the neo-race lens restricted the NHAS Implementation Plan from specifically addressing these needs.

This discussion and analysis of the NHAS is historically contextualized within the Obama Administration. After the Obama Administration, it is entirely possible that a new set of issues and crises will emerge, including if the NHAS is even used. We contend that regardless of whether or not the NHAS is still in play, the construction and use of race, particularly Blackness, within HIV public policy has impact beyond inclusion and representation. We argue that the use of CRT and intersectionality are central to being able to unpack, understand, and address HIV vulnerability and need for people of color.

In this chapter, we argue that public policy discussions must also have action elements that articulate the reality of the community in need. For the NHAS, the Strategy has a vision that the Implementation Plan does not always mirror. In this case, HIV stigma, Black gay and bisexual men, Black women, and people living with HIV are sorely underserved in this Implementation Strategy. Other populations—such as immigrants, sex workers, people who use drugs, and people who have experienced incarceration—also have specific needs unaddressed by the NHAS. Despite his best efforts, President Obama was unable to successfully realize the "end of AIDS" during his term. Until the NHAS addresses the drivers of the HIV epidemic—including social and economic justice, substance use and mental health, racism and homophobia, reproductive rights and gender-based violence—then we cannot reach the "end of AIDS."

References

Adam, B. D. (1989). The state, public policy, and AIDS discourse. *Crime, Law and Social Change, 13*(1), 1–14.

Bird, J. D. P., & Voisin, D. R. (2013). 'You're an open target to be abused': A qualitative study of stigma and HIV self-disclosure among Black men who have sex with men. *American Journal of Public Health, 103*(12), 2193–2199.

Calafell, B. M. (2015). *Monstrosity, performance, and race in contemporary culture.* New York, NY: Peter Lang Press.

Castel, A. D., Kalmin, M. M., Hart, R. L. D., Young, H. A., Hays, H., et al. (2016). Disparities in achieving and sustaining viral suppression among a large cohort of HIV-infected persons in care—Washington, DC *AIDS Care*, DOI: 10.1080/09540121.2016.1189496

Centers for Disease Control and Prevention. (2007). *A heightened national response to the HIV/AIDS crisis among African Americans*. Atlanta: U.S. Department of Health and Human Services, Centers for Disease Control and Prevention.

Centers for Disease Control and Prevention. (2015). *HIV surveillance report, 2014* (vol. 26). Atlanta: U.S. Department of Health and Human Services, Centers for Disease Control and Prevention.

Centers for Disease Control and Prevention. (2015b). *High-Impact HIV Prevention: CDC's approach to reducing HIV infections in the United States*. Atlanta: U.S. Department of Health and Human Services, Centers for Disease Control and Prevention. Retrieved 8/1/2017 from http://www.cdc.gov/hiv/policies/hip/hip.html

Centers for Disease Control and Prevention. (2016a). *HIV among African Americans*. Atlanta: U.S. Department of Health and Human Services, Centers for Disease Control and Prevention. Retrieved 8/1/2017 from http://www.cdc.gov/hiv/group/racialethnic/africanamericans/index.html

Centers for Disease Control and Prevention. (2016b). Lifetime risk of HIV diagnosis among MSM by race/ethnicity. Boston, MA: 2016 Conference on Retroviruses and Opportunistic Infections.

Centers for Disease Control and Prevention. (2016c). Lifetime risk of HIV diagnosis by race/ethnicity. Boston, MA: 2016 Conference on Retroviruses and Opportunistic Infections.

Centers for Disease Control and Prevention. (2016d). *CDC FY 2017 budget request summary: Domestic HIV prevention*. Atlanta: U.S. Department of Health and Human Services, Centers for Disease Control and Prevention. Retrieved 8/1/2017 from https://www.cdc.gov/hiv/pdf/policies/cdc-hiv-budget-summary.pdf

Cohen, C. (1999). *The boundaries of Blackness: AIDS and the breakdown of Black politics*. London and Chicago: University of Chicago.

Coston, B. M., & Kimmel, M. (2012). Seeing privilege where it isn't: Marginalized masculinities and the intersectionality of privilege. *Journal of Social Issues*, 68(1), 97–111.

Crenshaw, K. (1991). Mapping the margins: Intersectionality, identity politics, and violence against women of color. *Stanford Law Review*, 43(6), 1241–1299.

Cuomo, A. M. (2013). Governor Cuomo announces plan to end the AIDS epidemic in New York State [Press release]. Retrieved from https://www.governor.ny.gov/press/06292014-end-aaids-epidemic

Delgado, R., & Stefancic, J. (2012). *Critical race theory: An introduction*. New York: New York University Press.

Goffman, E. (1963). *Stigma: Notes on the management of spoiled identity*. New York: Simon and Schuster.

Herek, G. M., Capitanio, J. P., & Widaman, K. F. (2002). HIV-related stigma and knowledge in the United States: prevalence and trends, 1991–1999. *American Journal of Public Health*, 92(3), 371–377.

Holloway, K. F. C. (2011). *Private bodies, public texts: Race, gender, and a cultural bioethics*. Durham, NC: Duke University Press.

Maulsby, C., Valdiserri, R. O., Kim, J. J., Mahon, N., Flynn, A., et al. (2016). The global engagement in care convening: Recommended actions to improve health outcomes for people living with HIV. *AIDS Education and Prevention, 28*(5), 405–416.

Office of National AIDS Policy. (2010). *The National HIV/AIDS Strategy for the United States*. District of Columbia: The White House.

Office of National AIDS Policy. (2015a). *The National HIV/AIDS Strategy for the United States: Updated to 2020*. District of Columbia: The White House.

Office of National AIDS Policy. (2015b.). *The National HIV/AIDS Strategy for the United States, updated to 2020: Federal action plan*. District of Columbia: The White House.

Ojikutu, B., Nnaji, C., Sithole-Berk, J., Bogart, L. M., & Gona, P. (2014). Barriers to HIV testing in Black immigrants to the US. *Journal of Health Care for the Poor and Underserved, 25*(3), 1052.

People with AIDS Coalition. (1983). Denver Principles [Statement]. Retrieved 8/1/2017 from http://data.unaids.org/pub/ExternalDocument/2007/gipa1983denverprinciples_en.pdf

Pham, V. N. (2015). Our foreign President Barack Obama: The racial logics of birther discourses. *Journal of International and Intercultural Communication, 8*(2): 86–107.

Spieldenner, A. R. and Castro, C. F. (2010). Education and fear: Black and gay in the public sphere of HIV prevention. *Communication Education, 59*(3), 275–282.

White House. (2011). Remarks by the President on World AIDS Day. Retrieved 8/1/2017 from https://www.whitehouse.gov/the-press-office/2011/12/01/remarks-president-world-aids-day

Woodside-Jiron, H. (2004). Language, power, and participation: Using critical discourse analysis to make sense of public policy. In Rebecca Rogers (Ed.), *An introduction to critical discourse analysis in education* (pp. 173–205). New York, NY: Routledge.

6

The President Was Black, Y'all

Presidential Humor, Neo-Racism, and the Social Construction of Blackness and Whiteness

JENNY UNGBHA KORN

The historic election of Barack Obama in 2008 and his reelection in 2012 as the first Black President of the United States of America represented a cultural shift in political and social relations.[1] Within the public discourse emerged a different expression of neo-racism reflecting dominant and minority cultural beliefs about the holder of the highest office of the country. Rather than racism's emphasis on the characteristics attached to the color of skin, neo-racism provided the undercurrent to comedic discourse critiquing Obama as culturally inferior to the all-White, male Presidents before him, thereby preserving and reasserting that the Presidency should be occupied by the culturally superior dominant group of White men (Lee, 2015). Political comedians seized the opportunity to critique the historic change in the race of the President, using humor as a barometer for a new era in which "the leader of the Free World" was now viewed as an African American.

In this chapter, I centered my analyses of popular depictions of Obama's racial identity of Blackness through humor from racial majority and racial minority comedians. Specifically, I analyzed examples of political comedy that mention Obama's race, explicitly or implicitly, to study contemporary discourse on the behaviors reflective of and presumptions behind neo-racism and racialized difference. I examined the neo-racist biases that were exhibited in these examples of humor, particularly how racial stereotypes about both Blacks and Whites were referenced (Allport, 1979; Entman & Rojecki, 2002; Fiske, 2002). As racial stereotypes reflect ideology, comedy referencing race reproduces the sociopoliticized history of the United States (Bobo, Kluegel, & Smith, 1997; Ross, 2006). Therefore, in this chapter, I also provided context, particularly the race of the comedian, along with pertinent examples of political humor from Obama's Presidency in 2008 until 2012, during which the "novelty" of his race in his first term was popular fodder for political comedians.

Due to comedy's obvious lighthearted goal of laughter within popular culture, it is sometimes overlooked as a serious topic for scholarly research and dismissed as "light entertainment" (Brayton, 2009; Pickering, 1994). However, today's comedy may be understood as a cultural artifact of its time. For example, while rubbing a White face entirely in Black paint was once thought humorous by the dominant majority in the United States; today, most Americans would publicly disavow such blackface as racist (Pickering, 1994). Humor presupposes national attitudes about race and politics, such that specifically comic forms of discourse actually serve as heralds of changing, racialized American politics (Pickering, 1994; Ross, 2006). Political comedy in particular critiques power structures and cultural dynamics. Recent communication research on the intersectionality of comedy and race has focused on Puerto Rican television programs (Rivero, 2002), British fiction texts (Ross, 2006), British television programs (Pickering, 1994), and American stand-up from the 1980s (Daube, 2010). In this study, I detected historic and novel nuances reflective of neo-racism in the construction of race in the era of the country's first Black President, as espoused by comedians in their acts and in interviews that comics have given via television and print.

Online Political Humor

Utilizing the Internet for sources of political humor about Obama was aligned with and reflective of the time and culture of the Obama campaign and his consequent successful elections. As *The New York Times* (Hunt, 2012) and *USA Today* (Cofsky, 2012) touted, Obama's campaign had been highly successful in mobilizing young voters, especially in its strategic use of online social media. Thus, returning to the Internet for humorous effect placed source material back in the right context, one familiar to those acquainted with Obama's campaigns and strategies.

In addition, because of the nature of the Internet, vast repositories of political humor, jokes, videos, and images related to Obama existed online from 2008 to the present. In fact, ObamaJokes.com and Political-Humor.About.com had a combined total of nearly 200 jokes that specified the author of the joke and that referenced Obama, of which nearly 20% touched upon race.[2]

I view comedy as cultural texts whose content and juxtaposition between speaker and audience may be analyzed as representative of the context in which such humor is borne. In this chapter, I did not share the totality of all of the jokes referencing Obama; for example, I did not focus on jokes that reference the size of Obama's ears because those mentions are more reflective of a biologically based concept of racism, in contrast to neo-racism (Rasmussen, 2011). Rather, I focused upon comedy that represented specifically neo-racist understandings about the politics, history, and culture that alluded to Obama's race, both directly and indirectly. While citing racialized jokes that have been shared publicly in the internal comedy world via stand-up and television, I made special note when those Obama jokes move beyond the primary live environment to garner press attention as either funny or objectionable because they had violated social norms.

Informed by grounded theory (Glaser & Strauss, 1967; Charmaz, 2012), I identified examples of political comedy that specifically referenced Obama to illustrate how his racialized identity is constructed through humor rooted in neo-racism. The inclusion of such comedic material was not to identify its speakers as racist; rather, comedy is a cultural artifact of the racial, cultural, historical, political, economic, and social ideologies of the United States of America. Aligned with Allport's (1979) theories on racial bias and Bobo, Kluegel, and Smith's (1997) theories on racial ideologies, comedic discourse reflects racial ideologies that often manifest in racial stereotype and cultural difference, both examples of neo-racism (Hervik, 2013; Lee, 2015). Critical discourse analyses were applied to these examples with particular attention paid to power dynamics across different social groups (Van Dijk, 1993). This study contributed to a deeper understanding of contemporary discourse about Obama's race, political position, and his perceived cultural difference. This study also focused on how comedy helps to construct the identity and intersection of Obama as a Black man, Obama as a U.S. President, and Obama as a Black (male) President of the United States.

Political Satire

As Zoglin (2009) summarized, political satire in American comedy rose in the 1950s with Mort Sahl and Lenny Bruce; concurrently, stand-up comedy also began to emerge in the United States in the 1950s (Daube,

2010). Political comedy flourished in the counterculture of the 1960s and 1970s through George Carlin, Richard Pryor, and Robert Klein. The 1980s saw a decline in political satire as other comics, such as Roseanne Barr, Jerry Seinfeld, and Johnny Carson, became popular for "everyday" humor that avoided partisan jokes. With the backlash to political correctness and the advent of both of the George Bushes in the 1990s and 2000s, political comedy became popular again through David Letterman, Jon Stewart, and Bill Maher (Fairclough, 2003; Zoglin, 2009).

Among the savviest social commentators of the current, racialized environment were comedians. Political comedians are sensitive to the timing of significant events, particularly elections. For example, a joke about Sarah Palin when she was running for office is expected, but such a joke a decade later might not be as relevant. While comedy about presidents and other national leaders is pertinent, the added component of Obama's race proved to be a new lens through which neo-racist comedy was created. Indeed, presidential comedy about Obama specifically lent different insights into how perceived race served as an important filter through which people understood Obama. Obama was not just the President of the United States of America; he was a Black male President of the United States of America, and his status as the first and only such president provided a precedent into how comedians constructed a public, racialized, political persona of Obama.

Up to six months after Obama was first elected, he enjoyed a time of comic reprieve. The time between Obama's election and when political comedians began to use him as comedy fodder could be called a "honeymoon" or a period when the country was enthralled with electing its first Black male President in 2008. It could also be construed as a time for comedians to determine how to negotiate their approach to political humor and decide how to interact with Obama as a political leader of color. For example, shortly after Obama was elected, White male comedian Jay Leno remarked, "See, I got to admit, as a comedian, I'm gonna miss President Bush. Because Barack Obama is not easy to do jokes about. He doesn't give you a lot to go on. See, this is why God gave us Joe Biden" (Mike, 2012). To be fair, the timing of Obama's election in terms of comedic fodder was a difficult transition for comedians, with his race as an added factor. The eight years prior to Obama were filled with copious comedy about George W. Bush's ineptitude, such that a quieting of political comedy was almost expected after Bush's political opposite Obama was elected. From the onset, Obama's bid for the presidency as the first Black man in that office took center stage. Political comedians of different races bestowed upon Oprah Winfrey the "magical" ability to transform the presidency from White to Black: "There's nothing bigger than Oprah. Oprah can do anything. 'Betcha can't make a Black man President.' 'Watch me!' " The same joke also belied the historical barrier of Presidents of the United States of America as all White, up until Obama's run for the position (Zoglin, 2009). But as one blogger noticed, when the comedians started cracking jokes about Obama, then they were treating him as they would any other newly elected political leader (Mike, 2012). In other words, retreating permanently from cracking any jokes about Obama would be to treat his presidency differently from all the ones before him; returning to parody about Obama was to prioritize his office again as an appropriate locus for comedy.

Comedic Freedom

Comedians can say more than other public figures, often without significant regard for repercussion (Scarpetta & Spagnolli, 2009). As far back as medieval times, jesters were given leeway to say anything in "jest" and were sometimes the only members of the court able to voice an honest opinion about sensitive topics in local situations (López & Cadahía, 2007). Similarly, stand-up comedians enjoy a wide berth in their public representations of race, especially given the informal environment between the comic and an audience who implicitly has buy-in into that comic's success via ticket sales and selective awareness (Scarpetta & Spagnolli, 2009). Comedians might act as if they are colorblind in that they choose to bring up race with no problem because they believe everyone is the "same" (or fair game) when it comes to ridicule (Maquil, Demoulin, & Leyens, 2009). When asked about Black stereotypes and presidential humor, Black male comedian Paul Mooney's reply was indicative of how comedians enjoyed the privilege to transgress social boundaries, including racialized ones, while referencing widespread stereotypes: "It's not about chicken and watermelon. Black people like chicken. If chicken could talk, they would say, 'I hate Black people.' You can make jokes about everything. Nobody's safe [including Obama]. If it's funny, it's funny . . . There is no line. This is America where we can talk about our President . . . I'm a comedian. I make fun of everybody. I'll be making fun of you when you leave here" (CNN interview, 2008). Comedians enjoy a freedom in their profession to voice their thoughts in ways that would be considered socially unacceptable outside of humorous settings.

Comedic Freedom to a Point

What Mooney overlooked was the importance of the speaker of such jokes, as a Black person referencing that Blacks enjoy consuming crispy poultry is read, experienced, and understood differently from a White person expressing a similar belief, even within comedy. In other words, the meaning of a joke referencing a racial stereotype changes when the speaker is Black or White and when the audience is primarily comprised of a racial minority or majority (Omi, 1989; Scarpetta & Spagnolli, 2009). The issue for political comedy since Obama's election was whether its commentary was seen as politically motivated or racially motivated (or both). Black comedians faced a different barrier that Whites did not, especially when they engaged in culturally intimate humor (Cooper, 2007): when they took aim at Obama, some in the Black community interpreted such criticism as disrespect and betrayal by Black individuals of the first and only Black President (Braxton, 2009).

White comedians were strategic in poking fun of the racial boundary between good taste and bad when it came to incorporating stereotypes. In the following example, White male comedian Jimmy Kimmel represented White people that are navigating race in a post-Obama world when he asked Blacks in a barbershop about the acceptability of certain jokes about Obama on November 23, 2008:

> What if I make jokes about him putting rims on Air Force One? . . .
>
> Can I make jokes about him appointing Dr. Dre as Surgeon General?

Kimmel was acting as a proxy for White Americans who wondered how the comedic landscape would change regarding Obama's race. In the era with Obama as President, all comics had to decide how they were going to address Obama's Blackness, even if it was to ignore it entirely or construct it in well-versed stereotypes. Racially motivated humor, especially from White writers and comics, tended to be received as demeaning, patronizing, and neo-racist, and the veneer of comedy did not obfuscate its racial biases. The latter was the issue over which White comics like Daniel Tosh and Louis C. K. were attacked. Though their occupation buys them freedom in crossing boundaries, their race imbues their words on racial difference with the history and power of the White majority, replete with the legacy of slavery and anti-Blackness (Smith, 2012).

Comedic Freedom as Audience-Imbued

Yet Tosh and C.K. defended their comedy using a colorblind justification (Maquil, Demoulin, & Leyens, 2009), saying that their talk about race was actually more honest than others and that it was up to the audience to decide when they have crossed any lines into poor taste. Similarly, Black comedians, like D. L. Hughley and Paul Mooney, who touched upon racial stereotypes in their humor often, said that it was not up to the comedian to decide what was funny; rather, the audience, through their reaction, was the judge of the entertainment, including its potentially racist implications (CNN interview, 2008). Audiences were part of the collective experience of comedy, and the default was to allow wide latitude in experiencing comedy as funny, as opposed to offensive. Such a colorblind, self-acknowledged, free-for-all approach to comedy shifted the responsibility of comedic consequence from the comedian to the audience, which reaffirmed the comic's ability to say "anything." This comedic freedom also provided a strategy for contemporary humorists to ignore the socially determined barriers of political correctness: through employing the neo-racist language of cultural difference (not similarity) as a sign of political incorrectness, political comedians refused to be "polite" and engaged in "honest" communication (Esmail, Eargle, Lamikanra, & Armstrong, 2013; Fairclough, 2003; Hervik, 2013; Lee, 2015; Scarpetta & Spagnolli, 2009; Wagg, 1998). Again, because comedians were able to say "truths" surrounding racial difference that might otherwise be considered racist, their discourse with their audiences provided a uniquely sensitive, timely, rich, and candid portal through which race and neo-racism may be examined.

In a rare example of how an audience determined a joke as unfunny, White male comedian Bill Maher quipped after Obama was first elected, "Republicans were feeling particularly superstitious: 'They say the country is having bad luck because there's a black cat in the White House.'" Immediately, his studio audience erupted in loud groans and boos. In a subsequent interview, Maher defended his words by saying that his statement criticized conservatives more than it was a critique of Obama's Blackness. However, his audience interpreted his statement about a "black cat in the White House" as distasteful, focusing upon the Black part of his sentence as racially charged, even though "cat" is slang from the 1960s for a male of any race (Green 2005). In this example of color-based difference about the Black President, Maher's mostly White audience refused to endorse Maher's joke, reflecting their social understanding of Maher's particular racial depiction as not funny (Braxton, 2009).

American Racial Stereotypes

Traditionally, Black comedians have created humor from the pain and anger of interacting with an American political system that has discriminated against people of color (Braxton, 2008; Cooper, 2007; Daube 2010). Stand-up comedy also presents race as a publicly performative process (Daube, 2010), as comedians of color identify with stereotypes to create boundaries between races (Fiske, 1989), often exalting their own "folkways" as superior over others (Sumner, 1940). Comedy functions as a way to reduce social distance among races by allowing individuals to learn about the experiences of others, especially because Americans live in segregated societies which inhibit firsthand experience with other races (Bonilla-Silva & Forman, 2000; Cooper, 2007; Entman & Rojecki, 2002). In this way, political comedy often crystallizes and reinforces prevalent racial stereotypes in its spread of mutual knowledge in which widespread affective, behavioral, cognitive, and cultural differences among races are assumed (Fiske, Harris, Russell, & Shelton, 2009; Shelton, Dovidio, Hebl, & Richardson, 2009). In other words, comedians presume that audiences share stereotyped cognition (Allport, 1979; Banjo, 2011; Fiske, 2002) from which humor may be birthed. For example, Black male comedian Paul Mooney's aforementioned reference that if fried chicken could speak, it would say that it hates Black people presumes that audiences will draw upon the stereotype of "all" Blacks "loving" fried chicken. Political comedy involving race often borrows from stereotypes and then reaffirms those stereotypes as its basis for humor.

In an example reliant upon racial stereotypes, encouraging others to use blackface as part of humor would normally be branded as racist immediately (Pickering, 1994). In the Obama era, race in political humor was used to poke fun at how historically racist means for comedy were not politically correct. In other words, within contemporary humor is the pervasive belief that blackface is indeed racist, so "no" person would choose to engage in it, knowing how racist an act it is. White male comedian Bill Maher utilized this type of White awareness of past racist acts when he joked about a stoic (some said, lethargic) Obama in his first debate of 2012: "You know what the popular costume with the kids is this year? They get blackface and a Valium and they go as first-debate Obama" (Kurtzman, n.d.). But a danger existed in satirical humor, like this example, in that White audiences might miss the nuanced ridicule contained in the joke and through selective perception, would use the comic representation to confirm existing stereotypes, rather than question them (Banjo, 2011; Cooper, 2007). The latter was the reason that Black male comedian Dave

Chappelle left Comedy Central, as he realized that White audiences were laughing at him, rather than with him (Banjo, 2011).

Still other jokes referenced racial stereotypes with a casual, matter-of-fact attitude, like the stereotype that certain sports tended to attract White fans more than Black fans. White male comedian Conan O'Brien quipped on June 6, 2012:

> There's a rumor that President Obama will stop by today's L.A. Kings hockey game. He doesn't want to draw attention to himself. He just wants to blend in with all the other Black, Hawaiian hockey fans.

In the above example, the racial composition of a typical hockey game was taken for granted as majority White, and O'Brien's joke relied upon the cultural difference between White and Black audience attraction to certain sports: a Black man that attended a hockey game might be conspicuous due to the color of his skin. O'Brien's addition of Obama's Hawaiian upbringing singled out Obama not only as the rare Black man at a hockey game, but also the rare Black man in Hawaii. Yet, observing "Hawaiian" in Obama was not as apparent as seeing Blackness in Obama. By this joke, Blackness was defined by what it was not: a person that plays hockey and lives in Hawaii.

In an earlier version of the same theme, on January 23, 2012, Conan O'Brien referenced hockey again, but changed the focus of the locale from Hawaii to Indonesia:

> Today, the Stanley Cup champion Boston Bruins visited the White House. President Obama told them he loves hockey as much as any Black guy who grew up in Indonesia.

In the above example, the definition of Blackness was still tied to physical places where the stereotype was centered on the absence of Blacks: instead of Hawaii where African Americans were presumed infrequent, the focus was upon Indonesia, a country dominated by Asians, rather than Blacks.

The above examples about Hawaii and Indonesia containing few numbers of Blacks contributed to neo-racism in its conflation of race with nationality (Balibar, 1991; Hervik, 2013; Lee, 2015): Blacks were not illustrative of "American." When Americans are depicted in the media, they are White, not of color (Scott, 2010). The common criticism of Obama from his detractors about his qualifications as an American citizen took on a racist tinge as they questioned the American origins of Obama as a

Black man, not only when Obama was first elected, but again, when he was reelected. For example, in 2011, White comedian Jimmy Kimmel cracked, "These people could have personally witnessed Obama being born out of an apple pie, in the middle of a Kansas wheat field, while Toby Keith sang the national anthem—and they'd still think he was a Kenyan Muslim" (ObamaJokes, 2012). Kimmel also utilized sarcasm in a similar joke later when he asked, "What's the difference between Obama and his dog, Bo? Bo has papers" (Mike, 2012). Underlying these jokes was the neo-racist belief that only Whites were representative of America. Again, this criticism took on a racist element as no previous White President had had his citizenship origins questioned in past decades.

Other examples of political humor that used Obama's Blackness illustrated America's Whiteness more critically, particularly its politically conservative Whiteness. For example, Conan O'Brien remarked that "Tonight, President Obama and Mitt Romney hold their final debate in Boca Raton, Florida. The topic of the debate is what is more shocking to see in Boca Raton: a Mormon or a Black guy" (Kurtzman, n.d.). Here, the joke was not necessarily about Obama's race or Romney's religion as it was Florida's conservative Whiteness. Similarly, White comedian Bill Maher used Obama's race to poke fun at historically (overtly) racist Southern states when he cracked, "Obama is still ahead in the swing states and among women. He is of course losing among men and in any state where you can buy the Confederate flag in a mall" (Kurtzman, n.d.). The humor of that joke ridiculed neo-racists: the reference to the Confederate flag implied that those who would purchase such a divisive symbol were the same (presumably White) people that believed that Obama represented fundamental differences in culture between theirs and his. In another example, White male comedian Craig Ferguson implied that racism was a generational phenomenon and that older Whites were more likely to exhibit racist tendencies, such as believing that all Blacks resemble one another: "Today, Colin Powell endorsed Barack Obama for President. This news surprised many elderly Americans who thought they were the same person" (Kurtzman, n.d.). Yet, in a good example of how comedy was contextual, while the habit of confusing one Black man for another Black man was generally regarded as racist, White male comedian Bill Maher used that same strategy in drawing laughter when he compared Obama's lethargic performance to a depressed Michael Jackson in Obama's first Presidential debate in 2012: "Now we know what Romney looks like when he is all charged up. And now we know what Michael Jackson looks like on Diprivan . . . I have not seen a Black man look that disinterested and annoyed since I dragged Chris Rock to that Beach Boys concert" (Kurtzman, n.d.). In the same joke, Maher referenced cultural difference in audience preference to The Beach Boys whose concertgoers are mostly White.

Another example of Obama's racialized identity as expressed through comedy was rooted in language used to describe Obama. For example, "Preezy of the United Steezy" (Mike, 2012) reflected ethnolinguistic imitation of language typically ascribed to hip-hop and rap music, which are dominated by Black musicians (Brayton, 2009). In fact, in 1977, it was not just Black male comedian Richard Pryor's anger, but also his "street" vernacular that drew laughter when he appeared as a Black President on *Saturday Night Live* (*Christian Science Monitor*, 2008). Language is often a component of authenticity in creating identity; African-American Vernacular English may be a part of Black identity and is often the target of humor for White audiences (Bucholtz & Lopez, 2011). This type of comedy was neo-racist in its specific positioning of vernacular associated with communities of color as different from and inferior to the "proper" American English spoken by the dominant population (Hervik, 2013; Lee, 2015). This type of White linguistic comedy stereotyping Blacks as speaking African-American Vernacular English and as characterized as having rap "names" was in direct contrast to an intraracial, as opposed to interracial, depiction of Obama as a "BUPpy" President or a Black Urban Professional male that was educated at Harvard, who "looks like Malcolm X, and talks like Martin Luther King," as Black comedian Paul Mooney said (CNN interview, 2008).

Intersection of Class with Race

In 2008, Black comedians were hopeful that Obama's election might signal a social difference in Black-generated humor, moving away from comedy based on a victim mentality, in favor of developing more sophisticated humor (Braxton, 2008). For example, Black comedienne Patryce Harris remarked, "You'll see a lot more intelligent, observational, and middle-class humor like Chris Rock, and a lot less blue-collar humor like Martin Lawrence" (*Christian Science Monitor*, 2008).

One example from White male comedian Conan O'Brien touched upon the intersection of race and class and America's comfort with a Black president:

> Some political analysts are saying the 1980s sitcom 'The Cosby Show' helped Obama get elected because it portrayed a Black family in a positive light. They also say Obama would have been elected 10 years ago if it weren't for Flavor Flav.

In the aforementioned example, O'Brien blamed negative media depictions of Blacks for holding back American attitudes toward accepting a Black President. Specifically, his joke was a commentary about the type of Black that was popularized on television, e.g., Flavor Flav, a Black celebrity known for his outlandish apparel and old-school rap but was more recently celebrated for the two different reality television series focused on his romantic life (*The Surreal Life* and *Strange Love*). These shows presented an image of Black males that countered *The Cosby Show*'s portrayal of an educated, upper-class Black man who was married to a Black woman of the same socioeconomic status and who had a stable, thriving, healthy Black family whose life emphasized commonalities with White families of similar socioeconomic background. O'Brien's pithy joke actually summarized scholarly complaints about biased representations of Blacks in the media (Li-Vollmer, 2002; Mastro & Robinson, 2000; Mastro & Stern, 2003). In terms of neo-racism, this joke emphasized cultural difference between Blacks and Whites by contrasting the "exceptional" to its opposite: the joke perpetuated a narrative of the "good" Black male represented by Heathcliff Huxtable and the "bad" Black male represented by Flavor Flav; neither represents the totality, range, or reality of all of American Blackness. In terms of humor, Conan O'Brien knew that both Black men have sufficient renown publicly to make the joke "stick" (be comprehensible) to the dominant population; to the critical eye, his choices reflected how mass media are dominated by White celebrities over those from communities of color; the number of Black celebrities known by the majority is restricted to far fewer than those known by audiences of color.

By comedians of color, class was sometimes conflated with race (Hajnaj, 2007). For example, Obama's Harvard education was lampooned as "a very comfortable level of Black" by Larry Wilmore, *The Daily Show*'s "senior black correspondent" (Zoglin, 2009). In contrast, Black male comedian Felonious Munk took Obama's race and tied his Blackness to the stereotype of being debt-ridden and welfare-abusing in his profanity-filled, online video plea to Obama entitled, "Stop It B," in which he commanded Obama to "pay his @#$%& bills" (Editor, 2011).

In an example in which referencing race so explicitly would normally label the speaker as racist, White male comedian Bill Maher remarked, "But all this doesn't matter because Obama keeps pulling away in the polls. Every week, he gets a little more ahead. And with almost all groups. Liberals, of course, always supported him. . . . And conservatives like the idea of paying a Black man to clean up their mess" (Mike, 2012). Depicting janitors as Black men, but especially the President of the United States as a janitor, referenced class and race concurrently. It also poked fun at a

White comfort with people of color primarily in subservient roles to them, providing caretaking and cleaning. In contrast, and in an example that not even comedy may be a shield against some racist remarks, another White male comedian, Don Rickles, made a similar joke, yet was met with derision instead of laughter: "I shouldn't make fun of the Blacks. President Obama is a personal friend of mine. He was over to the house yesterday, but the mop broke" (Luippold 2012). Both jokes sent the message that Obama, as a Black man, was suited for the role of janitor, but not the role of President, based solely on his race. These jokes read as a way to secure the position of socially privileged identities for the dominant population on the basis of inferiorization of the identities of communities of color, reflecting and perpetuating neo-racist attitudes (Hervik, 2013; Lee, 2015; Pickering, 1994).

Racial stereotypes from the 1950s and the past manifested in the political comedy of the 2000s and now, reflect neo-racism in how Blackness is defined as the cultural "other" to Whiteness. Class is a significant, albeit conflated, component in racialized American identity. The importance of class reflects today's political period in that Americans might emphasize class as a more salient social division rather than race because class is not fraught with as much cultural baggage, i.e., the category of "racist" conjures detrimental, socially unacceptable images immediately, but the classification of "classist" is still ambiguous and not as deeply rooted in history as racism is. Because satire is sensitive to such changes, political comedy reveals truths about race and class concurrently (Ross, 2006).

Crime Metaphors

Comedians are in the unique position, as social commentators unfettered by common constraints on behavior, to critique political leaders with words that would usually mark them as problematic, or in some cases, even racist (Mike, 2012). I submit that this comedic content, particularly political satire, served as a unique dataset from which strategic observations of race were created and shared publicly. For example, White male comedian Jay Leno, in describing a public appeal by Obama's party to grant due time for Obama's promises to manifest, said, "The liberals are asking us to give Obama time. We agree . . . and think 25-to-life would be appropriate" (Mike, 2012). Now, while one could argue about the prison metaphor of Obama as positive (i.e., Leno meant that having a Black male President for life would be beneficial) or negative (i.e., Leno meant that Obama should be severely punished for what he has done in his Presidency thus far), the fact remained that Leno chose a criminal metaphor. In addition, though politicians are ridiculed generally as "crooks," the choice of "25-to-life" alluded not just to a common criminal, but to a violent convict who has committed a felony such as rape or murder to receive the sanction of a prison term of "25-to-life." Again, the neo-racist message was that Obama, as a Black male President, was not measuring up to his White counterparts that have been in the same position.

In another instance of political comedy comparing Obama to crime, David Letterman, another White male comedian, asked, "What's the difference between Obama's cabinet and a penitentiary? One is filled with tax evaders, blackmailers, and threats to society. The other is for housing prisoners" (Mike, 2012). Neo-racist references to Black men as criminals draw from the media at large, particularly from Whites condemning Blacks as the negative obverse of White cultural identities (Dixon, 2008; Entman & Rojecki, 2002; Gilliam, Iyengar, Simon, & Wright, 1996; Pickering, 1994; Valentino, 1999). The selection then to use a convict metaphor for Obama was not just about his Presidency, but specifically about his Presidency as a Black man. Using criminal references helped to spread fear, prejudice, and antagonism about Obama by highlighting and defining Obama's race as culturally inferior to the dominant population (Pickering, 1994).

The criminal metaphor could also be turned on its head by comedians of color who united in pride that Obama had broken through the color line in a positive way. For example, Black comedienne Melanie Camacho said, "This is the first time in history that a Black man beat . . . a White man and didn't get locked up for it" (Braxton, 2008). This joke spoke to the well-documented, unjust discrimination and penalization of the current justice system against Black perpetrators and White victims, sentencing the former to punishment unequal to the crime. In this way, comedy separated along racial lines often reflected a John Rawls-based theory of justice, particularly around injustices felt by communities of color due to distinctions made "between persons in the assigning of basic rights and duties and for determining what they take to the proper distribution of benefits and burdens of social cooperation" (Rawls, 1971, p. 5). Comedy then became communication in which anger and resentment against unjust systems of domination were converted into public entertainment and social critique.

This tendency to conflate criminality with Blackness led to issues regarding White conceptions of the authenticity of Blackness. For example, White male comedian Bill Maher made a joke in 2010 on his show about Obama's lack of authenticity as a "real" Black man because he did not carry a gun ostentatiously or shoot people with said gun in a campaign of inducing fear around him (Hip Hop Wired, 2010; Mastro & Robinson, 2000):

> I thought when we elected a Black President, we were going to get a Black President. You know, this is where I want a <u>real</u> Black President. I want him in a meeting with the BP CEOs, you know, where he lifts up his shirt where you can see the gun in his pants [saying]: "We've got a motherfu*king problem here? Shoot somebody in the foot."

The same quote above also belied neo-racist stereotypes of Black men as "angry all the time," a belief so common that Obama came under widespread attack for not showing enough emotion during his 2012 campaign (Hamby, Preston, & Steinhauser, 2012). Black comedians Key & Peele exploited this stereotype with their creation of "Luther, Obama's angry Black translator," a skit that President Obama himself enjoyed (Jimmy Fallon interview of Obama, April 24, 2012).

Racial Truths

Identifying Obama as the first Black President is not in and of itself racist. Obama is unique because he broke through a racial barrier for male presidents that had existed up until he was elected. The fact that Obama had been this country's only Black President was still relevant, even after seven months in office, when White comedian Conan O'Brien said on July 31, 2009:

> Conservatives are criticizing *Time* magazine because they put President Obama on the cover for the 12th time in the last year. Not only that—every week since Obama was elected, he's been on the cover of *Black President* magazine.

In this example, the issue was the worthiness of Obama as front-page material for a weekly magazine. O'Brien pointed out that the truth was that public attention to Obama was justified and that part of the public's fascination with Obama was due to his race. A magazine dedicated to White Presidents of the United States could choose from 43 other presidents, but a magazine focused on Black Presidents could only feature Barack Obama. The paucity of Black political leaders is real, but its urgency is muted.

Yet, at least one joke raised the possibility of a permanent racial change from White Presidents to Black ones. White male Ted Alexandro referenced an old adage about preference for partners changing permanently after experiencing sex with African Americans: "Not only is Barack

Obama our first Black President, but it's the end of White Presidents forever. Because you know what they say . . ." (Zoglin, 2009). This joke promoted Black sexual experience as superior over White sexual experience and then tied sex with politics. This humor relied upon the stereotype that a sexual encounter with a Black individual was so impressive that Blacks will be the favored partner forevermore. The hope in this comedy was that Obama's performance as a Black president would be so remarkable that all future Presidents of the United States would be chosen as Black by the American people from now on . . . unfortunately, the election of 2016 saw quite a different outcome.

Black comedians also made visible the fear (or cynicism) about any Black president getting shot by a racist White in disbelief that the country's president was no longer Caucasian (Braxton, 2008; Pareene, 2008). This joke had roots in Eddie Murphy's *Delirious* stand-up in 1983 about Jesse Jackson, and reappeared in Chris Rock's movie *Head of State* about a Black president in 2003, and again in Tommy Davidson's stand-up in 2008 about Obama (Pareene, 2008). The reality behind this long-running commentary was that people of color feared that racists would not respect the political process that justified the election of a Black president; rather, the concern was that the hatred of different skin colors by racist Whites would supplant a Black president's political position.[3] For example, Black comedian Mario Joyner remarked after Obama was elected, "You just know the Ku Klux Klan is having a big meeting right now" (Braxton, 2008). This fear was rooted in historical precedent with the assassinations of groundbreaking Black and White leaders, including President Kennedy, Senator Bobby Kennedy, the Reverend Martin Luther King Jr., and Malcolm X (Braxton, 2008). This assassination trope was unique to Black comedians only and did not appear in any White comic routine.

Comedians think about race in ways that others do not. In the following example, a Black comedian brought attention to a difference that Obama ushered in as a Black President. In an example of political humor by Black comedians that focused on cultural similarities among Blacks, Black male comedian D. L. Hughley quipped shortly after Obama was first elected that with Obama, "there's gonna be products in the White House that they've never seen before, like a pressing comb, a wave cap, a tube of Sulfur 8" (CNN interview, 2008). The emphasis here was on commodification of beauty products, specifically all hair-related, that were well-known within the Black community and were all items that Whites generally did not use. The joke was in the novelty that the White House would soon be occupied by Blacks that would bring not only their own personal self-care products with them, but specifically items representative of the Black community. This comedic comment was entertaining, elicited laughter, and countered neo-racism: it instructs and makes White America aware of impending cultural change that is different and maybe better, but definitely not inferior.

Limitations and Conclusions

Obama's election did change comedy across all races in the United States of America. Upon entering a new political era in which the President was Black, comedians were forced to negotiate with social boundaries regarding race, neo-racism, and the intersection of race with the presidency of our new leader. Both Black and White comedians remarked that they genuinely liked and respected Obama, which curtailed their willingness to joke about him (Ballasy, 2010; *Christian Science Monitor*, 2008; Zoglin, 2009). Some comedians admitted that it was easier to poke fun against someone with whom they disagree (Ballasy, 2010), while other Black comedians readily identified with Obama as "hopeful" and evidential of a loosening of social barriers against Blacks (*Christian Science Monitor*, 2008). The latter soon became an ironic joke as Black comedians snapped sarcastically that racism had ended with the election of a Black President (*Christian Science Monitor*, 2008). The reality was that the United States had made progress in electing a Black President not once, but twice, but having a Black President did not automatically, instantaneously, and magically eradicate socioeconomic inequality and legal injustice. In terms of humor, Obama as President did reveal a social construction, steeped in the neo-racist message that Blackness was culturally inferior to Whiteness, of what it meant to be Black (stereotyped in subservient roles, as criminal/angry/oversexed, as not belonging in certain states/sports/music, as not representative of America), what it meant to be a Black President (fearful of assassination, aware of racial precedent, hopeful of lasting change, especially future Black leaders), and what it meant to be White (slanted as conservative politically). Obama has affected multiple racialized areas of society, including comedy, and humorists provide insight into the social construction of race because of their comic freedom to tell truths in an acceptable way that is inaccessible to others; race continues to be an important lens through which comedic jokes deserve examination.

A limitation of this study was the scope of stand-up comedy only, which focused on comedians who have achieved an established level of public success already. Since they rely upon ticket purchases and advertisement sales, these comedians are constrained by the commodification of their entertainment. In other words, they must satisfy multiple public stakeholders at once, which might prevent even more racist ideology than what was presented here from manifesting in stand-up and late-night comedy. In a future study, I will contrast the findings from this research with politically motivated cartoons, especially from the conservative side, to analyze the construction of race from a different social basis. In addition, cartoons might lend a different insight into the construction of mixed-race individuals. In this chapter, I chose to focus on Obama's identification by comics as a Black American mostly because Americans relate to Obama as Black, not mixed, though his ancestry is of mixed ethnicities.

In this study, Obama's race superseded his political position: he was not just President of the United States; he was the Black President of the United States. Obama's presidency affected both Black and White humor, particularly regarding neo-racist narratives about race without direct reference to race. As always, that which is funny continues to be contextual and culturally rooted, and the race of who is saying it matters. Overall, the running punch line through all of these jokes was the same, though reactions to it run the gamut from laughter and surprise, to derision and prejudice: The President was Black, y'all. Indeed.

References

Allport, G. W. (1979). *The Nature of Prejudice*. New York: Basic Books.
Balibar, E. (1991). Is there a 'Neo-racism? In E. Balibar and I. Wallerstein (Eds.), *Race, Nation and Class: Ambiguous Identities* (pp. 17–28). London, England: Verso.
Ballasy, N. (2010). Comedian Marlon Wayans: 'Tough' to Make Jokes About Obama Because He's 'Trying To Do Something Good,' 'Sarah Palin Jokes Are Hilarious.' *CNS News*. May 5, 2010.
Banjo, O. (2011). What are You Laughing at?: Examining White Identity and Enjoyment of Black Entertainment. *Journal of Broadcasting & Electronic Media*. 55(2), 137–159.
Bobo, L. D., Kluegel, J. R., & Smith, R. A. (1997). Laissez-faire racism: The crystallization of a kinder, gentler, antiblack ideology. In S. A. Tuch & J. K. Martin (Eds.), *Racial attitudes in the 1990s: Continuity and Change* (pp. 15–44). Westport, CT: Praeger.
Bonilla-Silva, E., & Forman, T. A. (2000). I am not a racist but . . . : Mapping white college students' racial talk ideology in the USA. *Discourse and Society*. 11, 50–85.
Braxton, G. (2008). Black comics on Obama's win. *Los Angeles Times*. November 10, 2008.
Braxton, G. (2009). Funny thing about Obama . . . *Los Angeles Times*. May 4, 2009.

Brayton, S. (2009). Race Comedy and the "Misembodied" Voice. *Topia: Canadian Journal of Cultural Studies. 22*, 97–116.

Bucholtz, M., & Lopez, Q. (2011). Performing Blackness, forming whiteness: Linguistic minstrelsy in Hollywood film. *Journal of Sociolinguistics. 15*, 680–706.

Charmaz, K. (2012). Summer Social Qualitative Seminar, in person. July, 2012. Durham, NC.

Christian Science Monitor (2008). Black comedians adapt to Obama era: Is 'angry' out? *AZ Central*. November 26, 2008.

CNN Interview (2008). Making Fun Of Obama, Black Comedians Take Aim At The President, DL Hughley Chris Rock Paul. *CNN*. November 26, 2008.

Cofsky, L. (2012). Social media utilized with mixed results during campaigns. *USA Today*. September 4, 2012.

Cooper, E. (2007). Is it something he said: The mass consumption of Richard Pryor's culturally intimate humor. *The Communication Review. 10*, 223–247.

Daube, M. (2010). *Laughter in revolt: Race, ethnicity, and identity in the construction of stand-up comedy*. Stanford University dissertation.

Dixon, T. L. (2008). Who is the victim here? The psychological effects of over representing white victims and black perpetrators on television news. *Journalism. 9*, 582–605.

Editor (2011). Black comedian goes off on Obama: "Pay your @#$%& bills!" *IHateTheMedia.com*. August 11, 2011.

Entman, Robert, & Andrew Rojecki (2000). *The Black Image in the White Mind*. Chicago: University of Chicago Press.

Esmail, A. M., Eargle, L., Lamikanra, A. E., & Armstrong, S. (2013). The Art of Killing a Dream. *Race, Gender & Class. 20*(3/4), 64.

Fabiola, S., & A. Spagnolli (2009). The Interactional Context of Humor in Stand-Up Comedy. *Research on Language and Social Interaction. 42*(3), 210–230.

Fairclough, N. (2003). 'Political Correctness': the Politics of Culture and Language. *Discourse & Society. 14*(1), 17–28.

Fallon, J. Interview with President Barack Obama. *Vulture.com*. April 24, 2012.

Fiske, J. (1989). *Reading the Popular*. Boston: Unwin Hyman.

Fiske, S. T. (2002). What we know now about bias and intergroup conflict, the problem of the century. *Current Directions in Psychological Science. 11*, 123–128.

Fiske, S. T., Harris, L. T., Russell, A. M., & Shelton, J. N. (2009). Divergent social realities, depending on where you sit: Perspectives from the stereotype content model. In S. Demoulin, J. Leyens, & J. F. Dovidio (Eds.), *Intergroup misunderstandings: Impact of divergent social realities* (pp. 173–189). New York: Psychology Press.

Gilliam, Jr., F, D. Iyengar, S., Simon, A., & Wright, O. (1996). Crime in black and white: The violent, scary world of local news. *Harvard International Journal of Press/Politics. 1*(3), 6–23.

Glaser, B. G., & A. L. Strauss (1967). *The Discovery of Grounded Theory: Strategies for Qualitative Research*. New York: Aldine Publishing Company.

Green, J. (2005). *Cassell's Dictionary of Slang*. London: Weidenfeld & Nicolson.

Hajnaj, Z. L. (2007). Black class exceptionalism: Insights from direct democracy on the race versus class debate. *Public Opinion Quarterly. 71*, 560–87.

Hamby, P., Preston, M., & Preston, P. Steinhauser (2012). 5 things we learned from the presidential debate. *CNN*. October 4, 2012.

Hervik, P. (2013). Racism, Neo-racism. In (no editors listed), *Recycling Hatred: Racism(s) in Europe Today* (pp. 43–52). Brussels, Belgium: European Network Against Racism.

Hip-Hop Wired (2010). Bill Maher Cracks Jokes On Obama . . . Is It Racist Or Are People Taking His Jokes Too Serious??? *Hip Hop Wired*. May 31, 2010.

Hunt, A. R. (2012). Both Sides in Campaign Try to Mobilize Their Base. *New York Times*. August 19, 2012.

Kurtzman, D. (n. d.). Barack Obama Jokes: Late-Night Jokes about President Barack Obama. *PoliticalHumor.About.com*.

Lee, J. (2015). International Student Experiences: Neo-Racism and Discrimination. *International Higher Education. 44*, 3–5.

Li-Vollmer, M. (2002). Race representation in child-targeted television commercials. *Mass Communication and Society, 5*, 207–228.

López, V. R., & E. Cadahía (2007). The Court Jester in 16th and 17th Century Spain: History, Painting, and Literature. *South Atlantic Review. 72*(1), 93–110.

Luippold, R. (2012). Don Rickles Tells Obama Racial Joke At AFI's Shirley MacLaine Tribute. *The Huffington Post*. June 8, 2012.

Maquil, A., S. Demoulin, & J. Leyens (2009). Strategies for prejudice reduction: The norms of nondiscrimination. In S. Demoulin, J. Leyens, & J. F. Dovidio (Eds.), *Intergroup misunderstandings: Impact of divergent social realities* (pp. 173–189). New York: Psychology Press.

Mastro, D. E., & Robinson, A. L. (2000). Cops and crooks: Images of minorities on primetime television. *Journal of Criminal Justice. 28*, 385–396.

Mastro, D. E., & Stern, S. R. (2003). Representations of race in television commercials. *Journal of Broadcasting & Electronic Media. 47*(4), 638–647.

Mike, H. (2012). You know the honeymoon is over, when the comedians start. (Obama Jokes). *Free Republic*.

ObamaJokes.com (last accessed November 25, 2012). http://obamajokes.com/Comedians%27-Jokes.html

Omi, M. (1989). In Living Color: Race and American Culture. In I. Angus & S. Jhally (Eds.), *Cultural Politics in Contemporary America*. London: Routledge.

Pareene [no last name] (2008). Every 'First Black President' Joke Basically the Same. *Gawker*. November 10, 2008.

Pickering, M. (1994). Race, Gender and Broadcast Comedy: The Case of the BBC's Kentucky Minstrels. *European Journal of Communication. 9*(3), 311–333.

Rasmussen, K. S. (2011). Foucault's genealogy of racism. *Theory, Culture & Society. 28*(5), 34–51.

Rawls, J. (1971). *A Theory of Justice*. Cambridge, MA: Harvard University Press.

Rivero, Y. M. (2002). Erasing blackness: the media construction of 'race' in Mi Familia, the first Puerto Rican situation comedy with a black family. *Media Culture and Society. 24*(4), 481–497.

Ross, M. (2006). *Race Riots: Comedy and Ethnicity in Modern British Fiction*. Montreal: McGill-Queen's University Press.
Scott, T. A. (2010). Does American mean White? *Conducive Chronicle*. April 27, 2010.
Shelton, J. N., Dovidio, J. F., Hebl, M., & Richardson, J. A. (2009). Prejudice and intergroup interaction. In S. Demoulin, J. Leyens, & J. F. Dovidio (Eds.), *Intergroup misunderstandings: Impact of divergent social realities* (pp. 21–38). New York: Psychology Press.
Smith, A. (2012). Indigeneity, settler colonialism, white supremacy. In D. M. HoSang, O. LaBennett, & L. Pulido (Eds.), *Racial formation in the twenty-first century* (pp. 66–90). Berkeley, CA: University of California Press.
Sumner, W. G. (1940). *Folkways: A Study of the Sociological Importance of Usages, Manners, Customs, Mores, and Morals*. Boston: Ginn.
Valentino, N. (1999). Crime news and the priming of racial attitudes during evaluations of the president. *The Public Opinion Quarterly*. 63, 293–320.
van Dijk, T. A. (1993). Principles of Critical Discourse Analysis. *Discourse Society*. 4(2), 249–283.
Wagg, S. (1998). *Because I Tell a Joke Or Two: Comedy, Politics, and Social Difference*. London: Routledge.
Yue, A., & Wyatt, D. (2014). New Communities, New Racisms: A Critical Introduction. *Journal of Intercultural Studies*. 35(3), 223–231.
Zoglin, R. (2009). "Comedy in the Obama age: A hard President to joke about." *Time*. August 31, 2009. http://content.time.com/time/magazine/article/0,9171,1917717,00.html

7

L'homme de la créolisation

Obama, Neo-Racism, and Cultural and Territorial Créolization

DOUGLAS-WADE BRUNTON

> The pursuit of a strange and subtle goal, melting-pot, call it what you like, is the mainstream, though the unacknowledged tradition, of the Americas. And the significance of this is akin to the European preoccupation with alchemy, with the growth of experimental science, the poetry of science, as well as the explosive nature which is informed by a solution of images, agnostic humility, and essential beauty rather than vested in a fixed assumption and classification of things.
>
> —Harris, 1967, p. 32

Identity, at some level infers belonging—to family groups, communities, ethnicities, or nations. In the United States of the last 20 years, but particularly in the Obama era, the crisis of identity fed by neo-racist rhetoric surrounding immigration and national origin has arguably subverted the hyphen as a descriptor of pride in origin (African-American, Irish-American, etc.) into becoming a device of exclusion. This is predicated on Berger and Luckmann's (1967) definition of social construction in which "Reality is socially defined, but the definitions are always *embodied*, that is, concrete individuals and groups of individuals serve as definers of reality" (p. 116). As a result, the social construction of Whiteness as a consequence of *race-making* (Stanfield, 1985) has seen the interpellation *American* become the sole domain of those whose phenotypical features allow them to be assimilated into the construction of Whiteness that affords access to power and the means of production through the ascription of aptitude. Given this frame, there can be little doubt that since the Emancipation Proclamation in 1863, the construction of Black identities in the United States has been among the most debated and contested topics in U.S. society. Fanon (1952), in *Black Skin, White Masks*, alludes to the problem of race relations in the United States; locating it in the practice of hate that is not innate but is rather a learned behavior—brought into being by action and demonstration. He concludes, "That is why Americans have substituted discrimination for lynching. Each to his own side of the street" (p. 35).

So, if Harris's observation at the start of this piece is true, that we in the Americas define what polyculturalism is and have as our default setting the desire to confound easily identifiable labels, it would then follow that Hall's (1996) prescient observation that identity is not automatic, but rather, consensual and predicated on interpellation and representation is particularly apt. In this context, the election of Barack Hussein Obama as the 44th President of the United States of America in 2008 and his subsequent reelection four years later brought to the surface of United States society the assertion that "the politics of 'race,' racism, and ethnicity is invariably socially complex, politically and culturally contested, and historically on the move" (Cottle, 2006, p. 7). However, it is not Obama's election and reelection that became the subject of debate during his presidency, but rather, the manifestation of his personhood and identity.

As such, this reflection is rooted in the politics and constructions of identity as it relates both to people and to place. For the purposes of the analysis offered, reflexivity requires the location of the author's identity on Trinidad, the larger of the islands of the twin island republic of Trinidad and Tobago. With a social history of less than three hundred years, the island was spared much of the genocide that hallmarked the transatlantic slave trade. There is, however, a complicating variable in that, as with any immigrant society, reference to ethnicity in Trinidad and Tobago should not be made synonymous with race, particularly given that the third largest ethnic group in the country proudly identifies itself as mixed. Instead, I draw on Schermerhorn's (1970) perspective on the complexity of ethnicity in the postcolonial world. In this frame, ethnicity is constructed not just phenotypically, but rather through shared histories of origin or experience; a consensual consciousness of identity and what Schermerhorn calls "a cultural focus on one or more symbolic elements defined as the epitome of their peoplehood" (p. 12).

Through this lens we allow for the consensual identification of the individual in the context of this polycultural society, this polycultural space, as understood by all in society. Given the complexities of possible ethnic identities in a Creole space such as Trinidad and Tobago, the two major ethnic groups (Afro and Indo identified) continue to mine veins of distrust and misunderstanding as a means of controlling access to power. These veins of distrust and misunderstanding continue to be mined for political gain not only in Trinidad and Tobago, but, as became visibly apparent in the 2016 United States Presidential election—in the United States of America as well. Guess (2006) cites Kincheloe to make the point that even though there is no universal definition of Whiteness, there is universal agreement that it is a construction of power that is at once both monolithic and ephemeral—a social construction designed to control access to power.

If Obama's election and subsequent terms as President of the United States brought the complexity and contestation of race relations in the country into sharp focus through the means of his body and what it represents; it is the election of Donald John Trump as the 45th President of the United States, and in the immediate actions of his neophyte administration, that we see a continuation of neo-racism in practice as it works to "Make America Great Again." In a plural United States, the hyphen has been weaponized into a suspicious symbol and a tool in the disenfranchisement of significant groups of the population of the United States, in addition to questioning whether they belong in the American space—this defined Creole space. In considering time and its role in both racism and neo-racism, Wright (2015) argued for the examination of "racial categories like Blackness not as a 'what' but as a 'when' and 'where.'" In other words, race, its interpretations, and manifestations are not a fixed or known quantity, but rather ones constructed and interpreted in the same moment predicated on the lens through which they are viewed in that moment. According to Wright, this epiphenomenal moment of interpretation has been theorized by physicists as "indicating the primacy of the present moment, which is neither an effect of the past nor a cause of the future." (p. 41). This notion is shared by Walter Benjamin in his *Theses on the Philosophy of History* in which he sees time as an eternal present constructed through the repetitive nature or sameness of technology and society in the capitalist way of life.

Heidegger (1927) posed a provocative question at the start of his opus *Being and Time*: "What is the being that will give access to the question of the meaning of Being?" The concept of the dasein or selfhood of existence is Heidegger's answer to the question. For Heidegger, the dasein engenders three components of the human situation: being there in the world, being there as someone, and being there for a while. The dasein then is Heidegger's construct of the being for whom the question of being is important, the being for whom Being matters. Heidegger argues that for the dasein to exist fully so that it might actually understand Being—what he refers to as the "authenticity" of the dasein—it must first understand its relationship to time. The temporal nature of human existence is one measure, but this scale must be contextualized against the broader temporality of human existence.

Enter the Creole

While the Creole is not primarily a racial construct, the negation of place apparent in the move to make the term analogous with hybrid, mestisage and other biologically derived terms has done just that. Rather, the Creole is a technological affordance. At once both a construct and a moment of interpretation, the Creole is constantly negotiating time, place, and interpellations. Specifically, I read the Creole as the manifestation of Heidegger's (1977) assertion that the essence of technology is nothing technological. This phenomenological perspective allows for the appreciation of the genesis of Creole culture, people, and languages. Though there is nothing technological about the Creole and its milieu, the essence of this construct is inherently so. Captured in this construct is the history of the region, from "discovery," through genocide, slavery, and deprivation, to colonialism and the present postcolonial conditions the region finds itself in. As a product of the *Terra Incognita* of the New World, the original space of diaspora, of diversity, and of difference—the importance of Being is paramount in the construct of the Creole, as is the locating of self in place.

In the United States, the Creole is primarily bounded as a construct both historically and culturally within the borders of southern Louisiana, and speaks to the uniquely heterogeneous cultural landscape of the region. Of the space, Spitzer (2003) writes:

> South Louisiana society offers a powerful counterexample to the atomized "hyphenated-American" image of diverse, bounded ethnic groups [. . .] It also offers contrast to the idea that still lingers of a uniformly biracial Southern (and U.S.) society [. . .] This is a culturally Creolized region in a broader sense than the multivalent ethnicity of people actually called Creoles. (p. 62)

Though the specificity of this place and its milieu is at the root of the construction of this identity, it is also at the foundation of its present near irrelevancy as a lens through which to interrogate race relations in the United States. Dubois and Melançon (2000) make the point that in the period between the Louisiana Purchase in 1803 and the Civil War; the influx of Anglo-Americans into the region prompted a devaluation of the Creole cultural identity in the face of Anglicization and the growing distrust between Whites and Blacks.

That the Creole identity has become an addendum to the cultural history of the United States, it is important to note that the growth of popular culture and political awareness in the country owes a debt to the process of cultural Creolization that began in Louisiana. Building on the root of the word Creole, *creare*—to create—cultural Creolization describes the development of "new traditions, aesthetics, and group identities out of combinations of formerly separate peoples and cultures" (Spitzer, 2003, p. 58). When put into this frame, the United States was, and remains, a prototypical Creole space and its cultural products—jazz, rock and roll, Motown, and rap, among other forms, are creolized artifacts.

Demonstrably a product of new traditions, aesthetics, and identities, Obama has been termed "l'homme de la créolisation" [the man of Creolization] (Chamoiseau and Glissant, 2009) because he embodies the process of Creolization through his complex cultural, familial, and racial diversity impossible to fix in one static definition" (Loichot 2012, p. 88). In a speech in March 2008 available on YouTube, just after his assumption of the presidency, he draws parallels between his family's story and his hope for the United States: "[I]t is a story that has seared into my genetic makeup the idea that this nation is more than the sum of its parts—that out of many, we are truly one" (Obama, 2008).

Hall (1990, 1995) made the point that diaspora cultures, including those in the Americas, will always inevitably be syncretized. Speaking to Caribbean cultural identities and, by extension, to broader cultural identities in the Americas, he invokes four metaphorical presences *présence Africaine, présence Européene, présence Indienne,* and *présence Americain.* In this construct, the African presence is the site of repression, an echo of Africa lost to time and place, but present in every rhythm, inflection of language and, most significantly, in our relationship to time. The European presence, he argues, must not be located as a wholly extrinsic force, it is always visible as the very symbol of our modernity. The *présence Indienne* takes into account both the native First Peoples of the Americas, and the South Asians who migrated to the region. But it is the *présence Americain* that is the key for Hall in framing the Creole.

> None of the people who now occupy the islands—black, brown, white, African, European, American, Spanish, French, East Indian, Chinese, Portuguese, Jew, Dutch—originally 'belonged' there.... The 'New World' presence—America, *Terra Incognita*—is therefore itself the beginning of diaspora, of diversity, of hybridity and difference.... The diaspora experience as I intend it here is defined, not by essence or purity, but by the recognition of a necessary heterogeneity and diversity; by a conception of 'identity' which lives with and through, not despite difference. (Hall, 1990, pp. 234–235)

While Hall sets out a very necessary and useful frame on which theorists can construct their own interpretations of the Creole, and indeed many have done so, in most cases stopping short of naming the construct; it is the theoretical work of Gordon (2014) who, by interpreting Rousseau through the lens of Fanon, breaks with conventional thinking on the Creole as a hybrid, with multiculturalism as a desired societal ideal and with the binary of race as the default setting of life in the Americas, to present the most cogent construction of the political power of the Creole identity. This political power can be illustrated by the creole language that is the *lingua franca* of Trinidad and Tobago—Trinidad English Creole (TEC), in which can be found three distinct forms of the verb to be. That these forms and their use all can be found in and are constitutive of the TEC definition of the verb speaks to the sensitive and nuanced relationships that Creoles have with time and place—demonstrating the conscious importance of being-in-the-world for the Creole. In the vernacular of TEC, "you must understand where you come from to know where you are going." This hermeneutic circle is at the core of Creole identity, an ever-present reminder of place. The philosophical approach to temporality captured in this aphorism speaks to the consciousness of the Creole condition to time, place, and space.

In the *neo-racial* reality of modern existence but particularly within the United States, the seemingly dichotomous presidencies of Obama and Trump have forced into the open a social anxiety predicated on growing multiculturalism and manifested as a meta—or second position—racism predicated on the incompatibility of lifestyles and traditions, "cultural" distances, and the reinforcement of frontiers (Balibar, 2011).

The dichotomy between the successive presidencies of Obama and Trump is best encapsulated in Donald Trump's vocal and visible role in the "birther" conspiracy theory that clouded Obama's ascendancy to the presidency of the United States and has lingered to this day. Masking racism through the neo-racist rhetoric of speculation surrounding Obama's birthplace the birther movement stood on Article 2 of the Constitution of the United States, which prohibits foreign-born citizens from the presidency. The attacks began in 2008 during the election campaign, persisted through his first term, and gained positive valence with the entrance of Trump into the public debate in 2011. The sustained traction of this movement speaks to a construction of identity in the arguably Creole space that is the United States; that does not account for the role technology, its repercussions, and its manifestations have had on the development of the nation. By discounting and attempting to deny Obama's right to belong, the birther cohort weaponized the hyphen as it relates to people of color in the United States, making the observations of Teddy Roosevelt and Toni Morrison synchronous through the span of the more than eighty years that separate them.

> There is no room in this country for hyphenated Americanism. When I refer to hyphenated Americans, I do not refer to naturalized Americans. Some of the very best Americans I have ever known were naturalized Americans, Americans born abroad. But a hyphenated American is not an American at all. (Roosevelt, 1915)

> In this country American means white. Everybody else has to hyphenate. (Morrison, 2013)

It is difficult to fathom the consistent framing by the media of difference as measured against what have become labelled "American values"—religion, skin color, national origin—as a weapon or problem until one understands the social dynamic at play. This portrayal serves to keep people of color on the outside of society looking in and, by so doing, maintains a status quo to which everyone, on either side of the hyphen, subscribes. This is where looking becomes watching and where fear resides; this is what I am afraid of; this is what we should all seek to rectify. Since Obama's emergence on the national stage at the DNC in 2004, the right-wing media has targeted him and his policies. In June 2008, Rush Limbaugh, in reference to Obama's election asserted, "The one observation you can make about this whole business, because he proved it. I mean, it's—the growth of government started like crazy when women got the right to vote. Which just proves: Size does matter to 'em" (Limbaugh, cited by Aronow 2008). Unfortunately, the attacks were not confined to him. His family members were also often targets. In 2016, Fox News had to disable the comments section of an article about Malia Obama on its website after readers flooded it with racist comments. Responding to her acceptance at Harvard, these comments, like those levelled at her father, questioned her right to belong and attacked her morals, aptitude, and so-called "black privilege" (D'Onofrio, 2016).

In February 2018, more than a year into the Trump presidency, following the unveiling of the Obamas' portraits at the National Portrait Gallery, Fox News host Sean Hannity tweeted a link to a since deleted blog post titled "PORTRAIT PERVERSION: Obama Portrait Features 'SECRET SPERM,' Artist Joked About 'Killing Whitey.'" In an article appearing in *New York Magazine* reporting on Hannity's tweet, Eric Levitz makes the point that Hannity's headline seems to *more* than meet the burden of proof that Fox News typically applies to stories about how Barack Obama (and/or, Black artists he favored) degraded the office of the presidency (Levitz, 2018). Hannity's tweet did more than that though, it reinforced in the minds of his audience the notion of the hypersexualized Black whose lasciviousness, according to a 17th century theory recorded by Kendi (2016), is rooted in the relatively large nature of their genitals (p. 43).

In direct contrast, Fox News, and Sean Hannity in particular, have been very vocal and partisan supporters of Trump and his agenda. When Donald Trump descended the escalator in Trump Tower on June 16, 2015, to declare his ultimately successful run for President of the United States; the foundation of his platform was encapsulated in this infamous quote:

> When Mexico sends its people, they're not sending their best . . . They're sending people that have lots of problems, and they're bringing those problems with [them]. They're bringing drugs. They're bringing crime. They're rapists. And some, I assume, are good people. (Trump, 2015)

The foundation of his support was also cast. A frequent guest on the network before the announcement, Trump has been lauded by Fox throughout his ascendancy. When some elements of the media began to attack Barron Trump, the pre-teen son of the President, Hannity was among the first to rush to criticism of the attacks. In a radio show broadcast on January 27, 2017, Hannity went on the record: "I have these words for the media: leave the 10-year-old boy alone. Just like we conservatives left the Obama daughters alone. Leave the kids of politicians alone" (Hannity, cited by Bishop, 2017). A statement easily disproven. If Obama's election and subsequent reelection had been the manifest proof used to substantiate the argument that the world had progressed beyond race and moved into a post-racial idyll, Trump's pronouncement (and Fox News' continued editorial support) has since metastasized into a statement of intent for his administration, and is proof positive that hopes of a concerted change to the rhetoric of race, primarily in the Black community and predicated on Obama's presidency, were hollow and that the national conversation never fundamentally changed.

The March 12, 2017, Republican Congressman Steve King from Iowa tweeted in support of the rhetoric of the Dutch far-right politician Geert Wilders. King went on the record: "Wilders understands that culture and demographics are our destiny. We can't restore our civilization with somebody else's babies" (King, 2017). When pushed to clarify the sentiment behind his statement, Rep. King reinforced his position: in an interview on CNN the following day he proclaimed, "You cannot rebuild your civilization with somebody else's babies. You've got to keep your birth rate up, and you need to teach your children your values. In doing so, you can grow your population, you can strengthen your culture, and you can strengthen your way of life." Specifically, Rep. King was speaking about the United States' practice of birthright citizenship under the Citizenship Clause of 14th Amendment that, in itself, arose out of the 39th U.S. Congress reversal of the Supreme Court's decision in *Dred Scott v. Sanford*. The Court "found that 'a negro, whose ancestors were imported into [the U.S.], and sold as slaves' whether enslaved or free, could not be an American citizen." The Citizenship Clause, the first sentence in the Amendment, guarantees, "All persons born or naturalized in the United States, and subject to the jurisdiction thereof, are citizens of the United States and of the State wherein they reside." This is the pivot on which racism in the United States has been able to turn into a neo-racism predicated on the right of belonging.

Rep. King's statements echo those the Founding Fathers saw necessary to include the Three-Fifths Compromise that defined the status of Black people in the United States: Article 1, Section 2, Paragraph 3 of the Constitution. Arguably, this definition of the status of Black people as "three-fifths of all others" in the thirteen original colonies informs their perceived social status in these modern United States and, most tellingly, is rooted in what Wright (2015) terms the "Middle Passage epistemology." She makes the point that this epistemology is the knowledge millions use to tell themselves they "know" they are Black because they can locate their ancestry within this history (p. 44). Arguing that such narratives position history as a product of linear time, she warns that by locating Black ontology within this epistemological frame we run the risk of silencing "the contributions, viewpoints, and struggles faced by Black women, Black queers, and Blacks from outside the United States (and only sometimes from the Anglophone Caribbean)" (p. 44). She further argues that this epistemological silencing should give us pause as these oft-marginalized groups, in fact, make up the overwhelming majority of Black identities who understand themselves as possessing Middle Passage origins (p. 44). It should give us pause for two reasons—as noted above, linear narratives contribute to the silencing of marginalized groups and their identity construction and, second, it reinforces the monolithic Whiteness upon which both the reality of the United States and the right to belong in it are constructed.

As counterpoint, in marking the New World of the Americas as a wholly new world, *Terra Incognita*, place and space are mobilized, forcing us to negotiate with new eyes and with new methods the common spaces in which new cultures, new ways of seeing and hearing, and new meanings were made, and in which the dichotomies of our difference and sameness are located. By theorizing the Creole as both cultural identity and cultural space, Créolization provides a more accurate portrayal of the workings of culture (and identity) in the Americas than multiculturalism or hybridity. Both multiculturalism and hybridity are hegemonic in construct, acknowledging as they do the power relations across ethnic groups and the notions of permission and permissiveness. Polyculturalism, of which Creolization is a specific construct, acknowledges the roles of place and space and the negotiations of identity intrinsic in such unmapped or unknown spaces. It is this notion of polyculturalism that heralded Obama's rise to the White House—the hope inherent in his keynote address at the 2004 DNC in support of John Kerry. "Alongside our famous individualism, there's another ingredient in the American saga—a belief that we are all connected as one people [. . .] it is what allows us to pursue our individual dreams yet still come together as one American family—*E pluribus unum*" (Obama, 2004).

In this speech and throughout his presidency, Obama folded his family's narrative into that of the United States, virtually using himself as the example of what can be achieved with hope, dreams, and hard work. Specifically, standing on that stage in 2004, Barack Hussein Obama became the United States of America—in him was the culmination of the social, cultural, and racial history of the nation—it is the epiphenomenal moment that allowed the United States to see what it had created and to celebrate.

Since 2004, culture has responded to that notion with increasing resonance being afforded to minority voices across the media. The top box-office stars are hyphenated Americans; as are the most talked about characters on television and the vast majority of major recording artists. The media is also celebrating this notion of diversity outside of the entertainment spaces. National news broadcasts and magazine shows are increasingly being anchored by people of color—place has been found for mixed marriages in advertising, and some brands have gone so far as to use hyphenated, non-celebrity Americans as their major spokespersons. For Obama though, the epiphenomenal moment of the realization of the American promise came at a great personal cost. In attempting to negotiate his presidency through this conferred Creole identity in the binary construct of race in the United States, he ran afoul of both constituent groups who claimed him as their own. For some he was not Black enough, for others; that was all he was and that was not enough. Dyson (2016) noted that this "burden of representation" meant that Obama's presidency was the only one subject to epiphenomenal analysis because of what his body represented and the obsession with race in the national psyche (p. x).

Heterogeneity is key to understanding the Creole. Acknowledging the roles of place and space and the negotiations of identity intrinsic in unmapped or unknown spaces, the Creole is constructed not as the analogue, progenitor, or product of hybridity—what Kraidy (2005) sees as "the spirit of the times with its obligatory celebration of cultural difference and fusion [. . .] resonat[ing] with the globalisation mantra of unfettered economic exchanges and the supposedly inevitable transformation of all cultures" (p. 1) but rather as the named, constructed technological product in whose being can be found the resultant affordances of the various colonial projects that shaped the New World—including the United States.

This is a significant and telling distinction. As I have laid out in the body of this piece, the Creoles know exactly who and what they are—technological products of place, space, and time whose innate understanding of these phenomena resists the epiphenomenal interpretation of race and ethnicity constructed by the monolithic Whiteness on which the society of the United States is constructed. The monolithic Whiteness that marks difference with disempowering language that situates it as baseline, such as hybrid (which cannot reproduce themselves) and locates history in relation to the dominance of this construct. Identity, at some level infers belonging. It is constructed at the nexus of temporality, spatiality, and location—each of which contributes to its veracity. During the Obama Presidency the epiphenomenal realization that anyone born in the United States could ascend to the Oval Office became apparent *for the first time*. It shifted the clock of history, recalibrating it to the hard reset brought on by this moment in time. Regardless of the adjectives used to describe the presidency, Barack Obama and his person transformed the office by representation, seizing the epiphenomenal moment to assert the right of belonging of those whose access to the claim of belonging to these United States is qualified by a hyphen.

This structural shift in rhetoric has changed the national conversation around immigration and belonging. Inevitably, temporality and location have become rallying cries for civil society standing in protest at the neo-racist actions of the Trump administration as it seeks to "Make America Great Again" by bounding the United States with literal and figurative walls. Based upon the aforementioned reflection on the construct of the Creole, I suggest an identity predicated on place in a polycultural space. By this I mean identities that are constructed as American, no hyphen warranted (or weaponized)—identities located in the experience of being in the New World and accounting for all of the presences in the Americas. This then is what I see as the legacy of the Obama Administration, the ability to look beyond the obvious and to engage fully in the epiphenomenal time of the present.

References

Aronow, Z. (2008, June 2). Limbaugh on Obama: His "only chance of winning is that he's black." Retrieved from: https://www.mediamatters.org/video/2008/06/02/limbaugh-on-obama-his-only-chance-of-winning-is/143627

Balibar, E., & Wallerstein, I. (2011). *Race, nation, class: ambiguous identities*. London: Verso.

Benjamin, W., Arendt, H., & Zohn, H. (1968). *Illuminations*. NY: Harcourt, Brace & World.

Berger, P. L., & Luckmann, T. (1967). *The social construction of reality: A treatise in the sociology of knowledge*. Garden City, NY: Doubleday.

Bishop, T. (2017, January 27). Hannity Claims He and Other Conservatives Left President Obama's Daughters Alone, Here is Proof They Didn't. Retrieved from https://www.mediamatters.org/blog/2017/01/27/hannity-claims-he-and-other-conservatives-left-president-obama-s-daughters-alone-here-proof-they/215162

Chamoiseau, P., & Glissant, E. (2009). *L'Intraitable beauté du monde: adresse à Barack Obama*. Paris: Galaadé.

Cottle, S. (2006). "Behind the Scenes: Ethnic Minorities and Media Production" Module 7, Unit 39a. Master of Arts Distance Learning, Centre for Mass Communication Research: Leicester University. pp. 1–30.

D'Onofrio, K. (2016, May 3). Fox News Readers Bash Obama's Daughter with Racial Slurs, 'Ape,' 'Monkey.' Retrieved from http://www.diversityinc.com/news/malia-obama-fox-news/

Dred Scott v. Sandford. (1857). Retrieved September 9, 2018, from https://www.oyez.org/cases/1850-1900/60us393

Dubois, S., & Melançon M. (2000). Creole i, Creole ain't: Diachronic and synchronic attitudes toward creole identity in Southern Louisiana. *Language in Society*,

29(2). 237–58. JSTOR. Retrieved from: http://www.jstor.org.proxy.lib.umich.edu/stable/4169003

Du Bois, W. E. B. (1903). *The souls of black folk*. Chicago: A. C. McClurg & Co., University Press, John Wilson and Son, Cambridge, MA, Bartleby.com, 1999. www.bartleby.com/114/. [July 2016].

Dyson, M. E. (2016). *The Black presidency: Barack Obama and the politics of race in America*. Boston: Houghton Mifflin Harcourt

Fanon, F. (1967). *Black Skins, White Masks*. New York: Grove Press.

Gordon, J. A. (2014). *Creolizing political theory: Reading Rousseau through Fanon*. New York: Fordham University Press.

Guess, T. J. (2006). "The Social Construction of Whiteness: Racism by Intent, Racism by Consequence. *Critical Sociology*, Vol. 32, Issue 4 (2006), 649–673. CrossRef. Web.

Habermas, J. (1969/1989). *The Structural Transformation of the Public Sphere: An Inquiry into a Category of Bourgeois Society*. Cambridge, MA: MIT Press.

Hall, S. (1980). Cultural studies: Two paradigms. *Media, Culture & Society*, 2(1). London: Sage.

Hall, S. (1990). *Cultural identity and diaspora identity: community, culture and difference*. J. Rutherford (Ed.). London: Lawrence & Wishart.

Hall, S. (1995). Negotiating Caribbean identities. *New Left Review* I/209, January–February 1995.

Hall, S. (1996). *The Question of Cultural Identity*. In *Modernity: An Introduction to Modern Societies*. Malden MA: Blackwell Press.

Harris, W. (1967). *Tradition, the writer and society: Critical essays*. London: New Beacon.

Heidegger, M., Macquarrie, J., Robinson, E., Frye, N. (1962). *Being and time*. New York: Harper & Row.

Heidegger, M. (1977). *The question concerning technology, and other essays*. New York: Harper & Row.

Kendi, I. X. (2016). *Stamped from the beginning: The definitive history of racist ideas in America*. New York: Nation Books.

King, S. [SteveKingIA] (2017, March 12): "Wilders understands that culture and demographics are our destiny. We can't restore our civilization with somebody else's babies."[Twitter Post]. https://twitter.com/SteveKingIA/status/840980755236999169

Kraidy, M. M. (2005). *Hybridity, or the cultural logic of globalization*. Philadelphia: Temple University Press.

Levitz, E. (2018, February 13). Sean Hannity Uncovers 'Secret Sperm' in Obama's Portrait. Retrieved from http://nymag.com/daily/intelligencer/2018/02/sean-hannity-uncovers-secret-sperm-in-obamas-portrait.html

Loichot, V. (2012). "Creolizing Barack Obama." American Creoles, Liverpool University Press, 2012, 77–94. JSTOR, Retrieved from http://www.jstor.org.proxy.lib.umich.edu/stable/j.ctt5vjd80.9

Morrison, T. (2013, April 3). "In this country American means white. Everybody else has to hyphenate." [Twitter Post] Retrieved from https://twitter.com/mstonimorrison/status/319605083862081536?lang=en

Obama, B. (2004). "Keynote Speech Democratic National Convention 2004." May 22, 2008. YouTube. Accessed March 15 2018. https://www.youtube.com/watch?v=_fMNIofUw2I

Obama, B. (2008). "A More Perfect Union." Barack Obama. March 18, 2008. YouTube. Accessed February 18 2018. http://www.youtube.com/watch?v=zrp-v2tHaDo

Oyez (2018). Dred Scott v. Sandford. (n.d.). *Oyez*. Retrieved September 9, 2018, from https://www.oyez.org/cases/1850-1900/60us393

Roosevelt, T. (1915). Unhyphenated America. An address to the Knights of Columbus, October 12, 2015. Retrieved from: http://unhyphenatedamerica.org/2014/05/05/teddy-roosevelt-unhyphenated-america-speech/

Schermerhorn, R. A. (1970). *Comparative ethnic relations: A framework for theory and research*. New York: Random House.

Spitzer, N. R. (2003). "Monde Créole: The cultural world of French Louisiana Creoles and the Creolization of world cultures." *The Journal of American Folklore, 116*(459), 57–72. JSTOR, http://www.jstor.org.proxy.lib.umich.edu/stable/4137942

Stanfield, J. (1985). Theoretical and Ideological Barriers to the Study of Race-Making. *Research in Race and Ethnic Relations, 4*, 161–181.

SteveKing. IA (2017, March 12): "Wilders understands that culture and demographics are our destiny. We can't restore our civilization with somebody else's babies." [Twitter Post] Retrieved from https://twitter.com/SteveKingIA/status/840980755236999169

Trump, D. (2015, June 16). Transcript of speech. Retrieved from http://blogs.wsj.com/washwire/2015/06/16/donald-trump-transcript-our-country-needs-a-truly-great-leader/

UNESCO (2002). Universal Declaration on Cultural Diversity. United Nations.

U.S. Constitution. Amendment XIV.

U.S. Constitution. Article I, § 2.

Van Dijk, T. (2012). The role of the press in the reproduction of racism. In M. Messer, R. Schroeder, & R. Wodak (Eds.), *Migrations: Interdisciplinary Perspectives*. Vienna: Springer.

Washington Wire (June 16, 2015). *Wall Street Journal* Donald Trump transcript: "Our Country Needs a Truly Great Leader." Retrieved June 2015 from https://blogs.wsj.com/washwire/2015/06/16/donald-trump-transcript-our-country-needs-a-truly-great-leader/

Wright, M. M. (2015). *Physics of Blackness: Beyond the middle passage epistemology*. Minneapolis: University of Minnesota Press.

Notes

Chapter 1

1. For more, see Dorsey (2012) and Rowland & Jones (2011).

Chapter 4

1. According to Pew, "The average margin of sampling error on the 1,033 completed interviews with Muslims is +/−5.0 percentage points at the 95% level of confidence."

2. It is important to acknowledge the limitations in this question. This question serves as an important examination of to what degree one will identify as Muslim and offers them the opportunity to do so—by juxtaposing it with national identity. In an ideal situation, having additional questions to measure the degree of attachment and focus on Muslims, instead of juxtaposing it to national identity, which would serve as a stronger measurement to assess attachment to group identity.

3. In order to explore the propensity of Muslims to possess a group identity, I utilized a multinomial logistic regression analysis. This procedure is an iteration of the maxim likelihood-based estimation (MLE), whereby the dependent variable is categorical, and is inclusive of more than two values within the variable. Since the variable has more than two values, it necessitates utilizing one of the categories as a reference point. The dependent variable, in this case, is restricted to capture three cases. Therefore, the selection of "Muslim" is utilized as the reference category, utilizing it as a point of comparison to the likelihood of respondent's selecting "American" or "American, Muslim, equally" as answers.

Chapter 5

1. Woodside-Jiron, H. (2004). "Language, power, and participation: Using critical discourse analysis to make sense of public policy," in Rebecca Rogers (Ed.),

An introduction to critical discourse analysis in education (pp. 173–205). New York, NY: Routledge. This study follows the 1983 Denver Principles in using the terms "person living with HIV" or "people living with HIV" rather than "HIV-positive person" or "AIDS survivor/victim" (People living with HIV Coalition, 1983). When other language is used, it is in direct reference to a report or quote.

2. Seroprevalence is the amount of disease as present in a population based on sera testing.

Chapter 6

1. Throughout this paper, I use Black and African American interchangeably to mean Americans born in the United States that identify as sharing "Black" as a political, shared experience. I also use White and Caucasian reciprocally, and I choose to capitalize all four terms.

2. Other topics for jokes on ObamaJokes.com and PoliticalHumor.About.com included Obama's big ears, basketball passion, live-in mother-in-law, and his stances on gay marriage, health care, and the unemployment rate.

3. It is worthy to note that all of the Black President jokes involving assassination presumed that the elected Black President would be a man, not a woman.

Contributors

Douglas-Wade Brunton is a doctoral candidate in the Department of Communication Studies at the University of Michigan. A critical cultural scholar, he is broadly interested in the relationship between media, culture, and identity in a global context. This interest informs his research into the role online performance of self plays in the interpretive constructs of identity—particularly for people of color.

Omowale T. Elson, PhD (2001) in Human Communications Studies from Howard University. He is an Adjunct Graduate Professor in Communication at Stevenson University and Adjunct Associate Professor in Leadership at the University of Maryland University College. He coauthored a book chapter with Z. Green, "Unleashing Possibilities: Leadership and Third Space" in Carol Pearson, ed. (2012), *The Transforming Leader: New Approaches to Leadership for the Twentieth-First Century*, San Francisco: Berrett-Koehler Publishers; and "Gender-Agency as Communicated in the Intra-Interorganizational Structures of the Spiritual Baptist of Barbados: A Postcolonial Account of Cultural Resistance" in *The Howard Journal of Communications*. Dr. Elson is the former President of the Washington Baltimore Center for the Study of Group Relations, and former Board Member of the A. K. Rice Institute for the Study of Social Systems.

Heather E. Harris, PhD (Howard University) is a Professor of Communication at Stevenson University. Her research areas include the Obama effect, and representations of Africana women in particular but not solely. Her work has appeared in *The Howard Journal of Communications, The Journal of Black Studies, Business Communication Quarterly, Diversity Digest,* and *The Baltimore Sun*. Dr. Harris is also the recipient Stevenson University's Rose Dawson Excellence in Teaching Award.

Shanette Harris, PhD, holds the position of Associate Professor of Psychology in the Department of Psychology and is affiliated with the Program of Africana Studies at the University of Rhode Island. Her research centers on psychosocial and physical health concerns that impact the adjustment and well-being of African Americans, and also examines body image attitudes and eating behavior, gender role issues, and health behavior participation. She is a licensed clinical psychologist.

Zoë Hess Carney, PhD, teaches communication courses at Texas A&M Univrsity. Her work focuses on political and presidential rhetoric, globalization, and citizenship. She received the Rose B. Johnson Award (with Mary Stuckey) for her *Southern Communication Journal* essay, "The World as the American Frontier: Racialized Presidential War Rhetoric." Dr. Hess Carney's work has also appeared in *Presidential Studies Quarterly*.

Jenny Ungbha Korn is a doctoral student in the Department of Communication at the University of Illinois, Chicago. She is a feminist activist of color for social justice and scholar of race and gender in mass media and online communication. Korn is a Fellow at the Berkman Klein Center for Internet and Society at Harvard University. Her work has won the Carl J. Couch Internet Research Award, the Outstanding Book Chapter Award from the African American Communication and Culture Division of the National Communication Association, and the Outstanding Conference Paper Award from the Organization for the Study of Communication, Language, and Gender.

Tomeka M. Robinson, PhD, is an Associate Professor & Director of Forensics at Hofstra University. Her teaching and scholarship focus primarily on the intersections between health, culture, and policy.

Amardo Rodríguez, PhD (Howard University) is a Laura J. and L. Douglas Meredith Professor in the Department of Communication and Rhetorical Studies at Syracuse University. His research and teaching interests explore the potentiality of emergent conceptions of communication to enlarge our understandings of democracy, diversity, and community. His most recent book-length monographs, *Communication: Colonization and the Making of a Discipline* and *Notes from the Margins: Reflections on Regimes of Knowledge and Power*, were published by Public Square Press.

Nura A. Sediqe is a PhD candidate in political science at Duke University. She specializes in race and ethnic politics and obtained her graduate certificate in African and African American Studies at Duke University. She is a fellow with Duke's Center for the Study of Race, Ethnicity and Gender in the Social Sciences (REGSS). Her key interests revolve around the racialization of new minority groups and examining the political behavior and identity patterns for Muslim Americans. Ms. Sediqe attended the Honors College at the University of Michigan–Ann Arbor and earned her Master's degree in Public Policy from Harvard University's John F. Kennedy School of Government.

Andrew R. Spieldenner, PhD, is an Assistant Professor in the Department of Communication at California State University–San Marcos. Dr. Spieldenner examines health and culture in three areas: the body, HIV, and the LGBTQ community. A longtime HIV activist, he serves as Chair of the United States People living with HIV Caucus.

Anjuliet G. Woodruffe, MA, is currently an adjunct professor teaching Public Speaking at the University of South Florida, Tampa. She taught courses in Performance Studies and Public Speaking at Hofstra University prior to her employment in the Department of Communication at USF. Ms. Woodruffe received her Bachelor's degree in Communication Studies, and a Master's degree with distinction in rhetoric from Hofstra University.

Index

Affordable Care Act (ACA), xiv, 105
Alexandro, Ted, 123–124
Alger, Horatio, 5–6, 11
Ali, Muhammad, 83
Allport, G. W., 126
American Dream, 4–8, 18
American Indians, 3, 14, 17
Amos 'n' Andy show, 26
Anti-Retroviral medications (ARVs), 96, 102
Arab Spring (2010–2012), 44
Ards, A., 58
Asian American Legal Defense and Education Fund (AALDEF), 89

Balibar, Etienne, xiv, xv, 3, 76
Barnard-Naudé, Jaco, xv
Barr, Roseanne, 112
Beck, Glenn, 66
Benjamin, Walter, 133
Berger, A., 55
Berger, P. L., 131
Beydoun, Khaled A., 80
Bialik, C., 59
Biden, Joe, 33, 112
birther controversy, 60, 76–77, 95, 117–118, 136–137
Black Feminism, 94
Black Lives Matter movement, 3, 27–28, 105
Black Nationalists, xvi, 33, 38, 53–70, 64

Bland, Sandra, 27
Bobo, L. D., 126
Boundaries of Blackness (Cohen), 100–101
Brown, Michael, 27, 28
Brown, R., 57
Bruce, Lenny, 111
Brunton, Douglas-Wade, xvii, 131–142
Bryant, Carolyn, 28
Bush, George H. W., 29, 112
Bush, George W., 11–12, 81, 112

C. K., Louis (comic), 114
Caballero-Mengibar, A., xiv, xv
Calafell, B. M., 104–105
Camacho, Melanie, 122
Campbell, K. K., 9
Carlin, George, 112
Carney, Zoë Hess, xvi, 3–18
Carson, Johnny, 112
Catano, J. V., 5
Centers for Disease Control and Prevention (CDC), 96, 99, 105
Chappelle, Dave, 116–117
Chisholm, Shirley, 69
Citizenship Clause (14th Amendment), 139
Civil Rights Movement, 10, 16, 28, 57
Cleveland, Grover, 9–10
Clinton, Bill, 10–11, 32, 59
Clinton, Hillary Rodham, 35, 81
Cloud, D. L., 6

Cohen, C., 100–101
Collins, P. H., xv
color blindness, xiv, 113
comedic freedom, xvii, 113–115, 121
Congressional Black Caucus, 54
Cooper, F. R., 29, 32
Corker, Bob, 29
Cosby, Bill, 119, 120
Coston, B. M., 102
Cottle, S., 132
Crenshaw, K., xv, 94
creolization, xvi–xvii, 131–142. *See also* hybridity
Critical Race Theory (CRT), 94–95, 97, 98, 106

Davidson, Tommy, 124
Davis, D., 57
Declaration of Independence, 14–16
Delgado, R., 95
Dorrien, G., 24
Dorsey, L. G., 6–8, 14
Dred Scott v. Sanford (1857), 139
Du Bois, W. E. B., 59
Dubois S., 135
Dukakis, Michael, 29
Dunham, Stanley Ann, 37–38
Dyson, M. E., 141

Elson, Omowale T., xvi, 53–70
Emancipation Proclamation (1863), 132
ethnicity, 25, 27, 34, 132. *See also* race
ethnocentrism, xv

Fair Pay Act, xiv
Fallon, Jimmy, 43
Fanon, Frantz, 132, 136
Falwell, Jerry, 66
Fatherhood Education Institute (FEI), 42
femininity, 25, 30–36, 44. *See also* gender
Ferguson, Craig, 118
Few, A. L., 26

Flavor Flav (rap artist), 119–120
Ford, Harold, Jr., 29
Foss, S., 55
Fourteenth Amendment, 139
Frame, G., 31
Franklin, Benjamin, 5
Frazier, F., 33
freedom of expression, xvii, 113–115, 121
frontier myth, 4–5, 13–17
Fry, R., 3

Garfield, James, 9–10
Garner, Eric, 27
Garvey, Marcus, 57
gender, 5, 6 11, 16; Black Feminism and, 94; femininity and, 25, 30–36, 44; hegemonic masculinity and, 25, 30–34, 37–40, 44; marginalization and, 32, 39; parenting and, 36–45; race and, 27–29, 96–98
Germain, F., 68
Ghosh, Cyril, 6, 11, 18
Gilkes, C. T., 35
Goldsmith, B. E., 44–45
Gordon, J. A., 136
Gore, Al, 31
Grisham, Bob, 35
group identity theory, 84–88
Guess, T. J., 133
gun control, 13, 16, 17, 44

Hall, Stuart, 132, 135–136
Hampton Institute, 60
Hannity, Sean, 138
Harris, Eric, 27
Harris, Patryce, 119
Harris, Shanette, xvi, 23–46
Harris, W., 131, 132
Harrison, Benjamin, 10
hate crimes, 87
Heale, M. J., 4
Heidegger, Martin, 133–134
Herek, G. M., 101

High Impact Prevention (HIP), 96
Hill, E. D., 36
hip-hop music, 26, 83, 119
HIV/AIDS, xvi–xvii, 93–106
Holder, Eric H., Jr., 56, 81–82
Holloway, K. F. C., 105
Horton, William R. "Willie," 29
Hughley, D. L., 115, 124–125
hybridity, xvi, 3, 53–70; creolization and, xvi–xvii, 131–142; marginalization and, 61–62; multiculturalism and, xv, 132, 140–141

identity, 4, 95; cultural differences and, xv, 132, 140–141; group memberships and, 131; Heidegger on, 133–134; Obama on, 6–8; Rodríguez on, ix–x
Immigration and Naturalization Act (1965), 83
immigration policies, 17, 83, 138; health screening and, 96, 104
incarceration rates, 3
individualism, 4–8, 11–12
intersectionality, xv, 34–35, 119–121; National HIV/AIDS Strategy and, 94–95, 106
Iton, R., xiii

Jackson, Jesse, 60
James, C. L. R., 59
Jamieson, K. H., 9
Jarrett, Valerie, 55, 80–81
jazz music, 135
Jentleson, B., 32
Jim Crow laws, x, 67
Johnson, Lyndon B., 10
Jones, J. M., 7, 12, 46
Jordan, Barbara, 69

Keni, I. X., 138
Kennedy, Jacqueline, 35
Kennedy, John F., 31, 124
Kennedy, Robert F., 124

Kerry, John, 31, 140
Kimmel, Jimmy, 114
Kimmel, M., 102
King, Martin Luther, Jr., 3, 68, 124
King, Steve, 139
Klein, Robert, 112
Kochhar, R., 3
Korn, Jenny Ungbha, xvii, 109–126
Kraidy, M. M., 141
Kupchan, C., 32

Lawrence, K. S., 44
Lawrence, Martin, 119
Lee, J., xiv–xv
Leno, Jay, 112, 121–122
Letterman, David, 112, 122
Levitz, Eric, 138
Lewis, L., 57
LGBTQ communities, xv, 39, 70; marriage equality and, 16–17; National HIV/AIDS Strategy and, 93–106
Limbaugh, Rush, 66, 137
Loichot, V., 135
Luckman, T., 131
lynching, 14, 28, 132

Macon, Marc, 68
Maher, Bill, 112, 115, 116, 118–123
Malcolm X, 33, 68, 83, 124
Manning, M., 57, 59
marginalization, 24, 140; First Ladies and, 35; gender roles and, 32, 39; HIV/AIDS and, 94, 97, 103–105; hybridity and, 61–62; Iton on, xiii; political power and, 53–54; racial stereotypes and, 29, 32–33; of White supremacists, 65
marriage equality, 16–17
Martin, Trayvon, 7, 27–28
masculinity, 5, 6 11; hegemonic, 25, 30–34, 37–40, 44; parenting and, 37–45; transformational, xvi, 23–46. *See also* gender

McCain, John, 79–80
McConnell, Mitch, 66
Melançon, M., 135
men who have sex with men (MSM), 96–98, 101
Michaux, M. B., 23
Middle Passage, 139–140
Million Men March (MMM), 58
Mills, C., 56
mixed race. *See* hybridity
Mooney, Paul, 113–116, 119
Morrison, Toni, 137
Moynihan, Daniel Patrick, 33
multiculturalism, xv, 132, 140–141
multinomial logistic regression analysis, 145n3
Munk, Felonious, 120
Murphy, Eddie, 124
Murphy, Troy, 11
Muslims, xv, xvi, 75–88; group identity among, x, 86–87
Muwakkil, S., 58
My Brother's Keeper program, 43

Napolitano, Janet, 81
Nation of Islam, 57, 82–83
National HIV/AIDS Strategy (NHAS), xvi–xvii, 93–106
National Security Entry-Exit Registration System (NSEERS), 81
neoliberalism, 64, 95, 96, 106
neo-racism, 139; Balibar on, 3; creolization and, 131–142; definitions of, xiv–xv; hybridity and, 53–70, 135–136; intersectionality and, xv; Obama jokes and, xvii, 109–126, 146n2; post-racial society and, 4. *See also* post-racial society
Nixon, Richard M., 11

Obama, Barack, xvi; on American Dream, 6–8, 18; *The Audacity of Hope* by, 7; birther controversy about, 60, 76–77, 95, 117–118, 136–137; Black Lives Matter movement and, 105; Carney on, 3–18; comedy about, xvii, 109–126, 146n2; creolization and, 53–70, 135–136; Democratic Convention address of, 12; *Dreams from My Father* by, 37, 60; inaugural addresses of, 9–18; National HIV/AIDS Strategy and, 93–106; on parenting, 37–45; portrait of, 138; State of the Union Address by, 45; transformational masculinity and, 23–46
Obama, Malia, 24, 45, 138
Obama, Michelle, xvi, 23–24, 34–36, 45–46, 62, 138
Obama, Sasha, 24, 45
"Obama effect," 46
Obamacare (Affordable Care Act), xiv, 105
O'Brien, Conan, 117–120, 123
Office of National AIDS Policy (ONAP), 93
Onassis, Jacqueline Kennedy, 35

Palin, Sarah, 112
Parry-Giles, T., 10
Patriot Act, 81
Pinckney, Clementa, 7–8
pioneer myth, 4–5, 13–17
Posey, Sean, 60
post-racial society, x, xiv, 4, 138–139. *See also* neo-racism
Powell, Colin, 80, 118
Pre-Exposure Prophylaxis (PrEP), 96
President's Emergency Plan for AIDS Relief (PEPFAR), 94
Price, M., 59
prison populations, 3
Pryor, Richard, 112, 119
public health, "trickle-down," 104

race, 17; class and, 119–121; ethnicity and, 25, 27, 34, 132; gender and, 27–29, 96–98; sexuality and, 28–29,

96–98; social construction of, 24–25, 131–132
Ramadan, Tariq, 81
Ransaw, T., 44
rap music, 26, 119–120, 135
Rawls, John, 122
Reagan, Ronald, 11, 31, 44
Reid, J., 55
Responsible Fatherhood and Healthy Families Act, 42
Rice, C., xiv–xv
Rice, Susan, 56
Rice, Tamir, 27
Rickles, Don, 121
Riley, Jason, x
Robinson, Tomeka M., xvi–xvii, 93–106
Rock, Chris, 119, 124
rock and roll music, 135
Rodríguez, Amardo, ix–x
Romney, Mitt, 118
Roof, Dylann, 30
Roosevelt, Theodore, 137
Rowland, R.C., 7, 12, 46
Russell, K., 62

Sahl, Mort, 111
satire, political, 111–113, 121
Schermerhorn, R. A., 132
Sediqe, Nura, xvi, 75–88
Seinfeld, Jerry, 112
September 11, 2001, attacks, 11–12, 78
seroprevalence, 96, 146n2
slavery, x, 15, 23, 114; *Dred Scott* decision on, 139; Muslims and, 82; racial stereotypes and, 25–29, 32–33; in Trinidad, 132, 134
Slotkin, Richard, 13–14
Smiley, Tavis, 66
social constructionism, 24–25, 131–132
Soetoro, Lolo, 38
Spieldenner, Andrew R., xvi–xvii, 93–106

Spitzer, N. R., 134–135
Squires, C., xiv
Steele, S., 62
Stefancic, J., 95
Stein, Ben, 27–28
Stephens, D. P., 26
stereotypes, racial, 32–33, 35–36; jokes about, xvii, 110, 114, 116–119; slavery effects on, 25–29
Stewart, Charles "Chuck," 29
Stewart, Jon, 112, 120
Strong Fathers, Strong Families program, 42
Stuckey, Mary E., 14, 17
Sullivan, A., 44

Talley, Andre Leon, 36
Till, Emmet, 28
tokenism, 6
Tosh, Daniel, 114
"trickle-down public health" policies, 104
Trinidad and Tobago, xvii, 132–133, 136
Trump, Barron, 138
Trump, Donald, 66, 138–139, 142; birther movement and, 76–77, 136
Turner, Frederick Jackson, 13
Tyson, Timothy, 28

United States Sentencing Commission, 3

voting rights, 9, 10, 16, 17

Wallerstein, Immanuel, xiv
"We Shall Overcome" (anthem), 10
Wells, Ida B., 28
Wells, L., 56, 66
West, Cornel, 60, 66, 68, 69
Wilders, Geert, 139
Wilmore, Larry, 120
Wilson, K. H., 10–11

Winfrey, Oprah, 113
Winter, N. J. G., 31
women suffrage, 16
Woodruffe, Anjuliet, xvi–xvii, 93–106
Woods, Tiger, 68
Woodside-Jiron, H., 95
World AIDS Day, 93, 105

Wright, Jeremiah, Jr., 63
Wright, M. M., 133, 139

Young, G., 60–61

Zimmerman, George, 7, 27
Zoglin, R., 111

www.ingramcontent.com/pod-product-compliance
Lightning Source LLC
Chambersburg PA
CBHW030828230426
43667CB00008B/1422